MznLnx

Missing Links Exam Preps

Exam Prep for

Contemporary Management

Jones & George, 6th Edition

The MznLnx Exam Prep is your link from the texbook and lecture to your exams.
The MznLnx Exam Preps are unauthorized and comprehensive reviews of your textbooks.

All material provided by MznLnx and Rico Publications (c) 2010
Textbook publishers and textbook authors do not particpate in or contribute to these reviews.

MznLnx

Rico Publications

Exam Prep for Contemporary Management
6th Edition
Jones & George

Publisher: Raymond Houge
Assistant Editor: Michael Rouger
Text and Cover Designer: Lisa Buckner
Marketing Manager: Sara Swagger
Project Manager, Editorial Production: Jerry Emerson
Art Director: Vernon Lowerui

Product Manager: Dave Mason
Editorial Assitant: Rachel Guzmanji
Pedagogy: Debra Long
Cover Image: Jim Reed/Getty Images
Text and Cover Printer: City Printing, Inc.
Compositor: Media Mix, Inc.

(c) 2010 Rico Publications
ALL RIGHTS RESERVED. No part of this work covered by the copyright may be reproduced or used in any form or by an means--graphic, electronic, or mechanical, including photocopying, recording, taping, Web distribution, information storage, and retrieval systems, or in any other manner--without the written permission of the publisher.

Printed in the United States
ISBN:

> For more information about our products, contact us at:
> Dave.Mason@RicoPublications.com
>
> For permission to use material from this text or product, submit a request online to:
> Dave.Mason@RicoPublications.com

Contents

CHAPTER 1
Managers and Managing — 1

CHAPTER 2
The Evolution of Management Thought — 6

CHAPTER 3
Values, Attitudes, Emotions, and Culture: The Manager as a Person — 12

CHAPTER 4
Ethics and Social Responsibility — 17

CHAPTER 5
Managing Diverse Employees in a Multicultural Environment — 19

CHAPTER 6
Managing in the Global Environment — 24

CHAPTER 7
Decision Making, Learning, Creativity, and Entrepreneurship — 28

CHAPTER 8
The Manager as a Planner and Strategist — 34

CHAPTER 9
Value-Chain Management: Functional Strategies for Competitive Advantage — 39

CHAPTER 10
Managing Organizational Structure and Culture — 45

CHAPTER 11
Organizational Control and Change — 52

CHAPTER 12
Human Resource Management — 56

CHAPTER 13
Motivation and Performance — 67

CHAPTER 14
Leadership — 74

CHAPTER 15
Effective Groups and Teams — 77

CHAPTER 16
Promoting Effective Communication — 80

CHAPTER 17
Managing Conflict, Politics, and Negotiation — 82

CHAPTER 18
Using Advanced Information Technology to Increase Performance — 84

ANSWER KEY — 90

TO THE STUDENT

COMPREHENSIVE

The *MznLnx* Exam Prep series is designed to help you pass your exams. Editors at MznLnx review your textbooks and then prepare these practice exams to help you master the textbook material. Unlike study guides, workbooks, and practice tests provided by the texbook publisher and textbook authors, *MznLnx* gives you **all** of the material in each chapter in exam form, not just samples, so you can be sure to nail your exam.

MECHANICAL

The MznLnx Exam Prep series creates exams that will help you learn the subject matter as well as test you on your understanding. Each question is designed to help you master the concept. Just working through the exams, you gain an understanding of the subject--its a simple mechanical process that produces success.

INTEGRATED STUDY GUIDE AND REVIEW

MznLnx is not just a set of exams designed to test you, its also a comprehensive review of the subject content. Each exam question is also a review of the concept, making sure that you will get the answer correct without having to go to other sources of material. You learn as you go! Its the easiest way to pass an exam.

HUMOR

Studying can be tedious and dry. MznLnx's instructional design includes moderate humor within the exam questions on occassion, to break the tedium and revitalize the brain

Chapter 1. Managers and Managing

1. _____ comprises the actual output or results of an organization as measured against its intended outputs (or goals and objectives.)

Specialists in many fields are concerned with _____ including strategic planners, operations, finance, legal, and organizational development.

In recent years, many organizations have attempted to manage _____ using the balanced scorecard methodology where performance is tracked and measured in multiple dimensions such as:

- financial performance (e.g. shareholder return)
- customer service
- social responsibility (e.g. corporate citizenship, community outreach)
- employee stewardship

a. A4e
b. Organizational performance
c. A Stake in the Outcome
d. AAAI

2. An _____ is a mostly hierarchical concept of subordination of entities that collaborate and contribute to serve one common aim.

Organizations are a variant of clustered entities. The structure of an organization is usually set up in many a styles, dependent on their objectives and ambience.

a. Open shop
b. Organizational development
c. Informal organization
d. Organizational structure

3. An _____ is a person who has possession of an enterprise and assumes significant accountability for the inherent risks and the outcome. It is an ambitious leader who combines land, labor, and capital to create and market new goods or services. The term is a loanword from French and was first defined by the Irish economist Richard Cantillon.

a. Entrepreneur
b. A Stake in the Outcome
c. AAAI
d. A4e

Chapter 1. Managers and Managing

4. In politics, a _____, (by metaphor with the carved _____ at the prow of a sailing ship), is a person who holds an important title or office yet executes little actual power, most commonly limited by convention rather than law. Common _____s include constitutional monarchs, such as: Queen Elizabeth II, the Emperor of Japan, or presidents in parliamentary democracies, such as the President of Israel.

While the authority of a _____ is in practice generally symbolic, public opinion, respect for the office or the office holder and access to high levels of government can give them significant influence on events.

   a. 33 Strategies of War
   b. 28-hour day
   c. 1990 Clean Air Act
   d. Figurehead

5. A chief executive officer (_____) or chief executive is one of the highest-ranking corporate officer (executive) or administrator in charge of total management. An individual selected as President and _____ of a corporation, company, organization, or agency, reports to the board of directors. In internal communication and press releases, many companies capitalize the term and those of other high positions, even when they are not proper nouns.
   a. Chief executive officer
   b. Portfolio manager
   c. CEO
   d. Director of communications

6. A _____ or chief executive is one of the highest-ranking corporate officer (executive) or administrator in charge of total management. An individual selected as President and _____ of a corporation, company, organization, or agency, reports to the board of directors. In internal communication and press releases, many companies capitalize the term and those of other high positions, even when they are not proper nouns.
   a. Financial analyst
   b. Purchasing manager
   c. Chief brand officer
   d. Chief executive officer

7. A _____ or chief operations officer is a corporate officer responsible for managing the day-to-day activities of the corporation and for operations management (OM.) The _____ is one of the highest-ranking members of an organization's senior management, monitoring the daily operations of the company and reporting to the board of directors and the top executive officer, usually the chief executive officer (CEO.) The _____ is usually an executive or senior officer.

a. Supervisory board
b. Product innovation
c. Value based pricing
d. Chief operating officer

8. While _____ literally refers to a person responsible for the performance of duties involved in running an organization, the exact meaning of the role is variable, depending on the organization.

While there is no clear line between executive or principal and inferior officers, principal officers are high-level officials in the executive branch of U.S. government such as department heads of independent agencies. In Humphrey's Executor v. United States, 295 U.S. 602 (1935), the Court distinguished between _____s and quasi-legislative or quasi-judicial officers by stating that the former serve at the pleasure of the President and may be removed at his discretion.

a. Australian Fair Pay and Conditions Standard
b. Unreported employment
c. Easement
d. Executive officer

9. _____ is something that a firm can do well and that meets the following three conditions:

Competencies are things that companys execute well across several business units or product sectors.

Firms usually have few competencies, but these are usually less liable to change rapidly.

1. It provides consumer benefits
2. It is not easy for competitors to imitate
3. It can be leveraged widely to many products and markets.

A _____ can take various forms, including technical/subject matter know-how, a reliable process and/or close relationships with customers and suppliers (Mascarenhas et al. 1998.)

a. Dominant Design
b. Core competency
c. NAIRU
d. Learning-by-doing

Chapter 1. Managers and Managing

10. _____ is subcontracting a process, such as product design or manufacturing, to a third-party company. The decision to outsource is often made in the interest of lowering cost or making better use of time and energy costs, redirecting or conserving energy directed at the competencies of a particular business, or to make more efficient use of land, labor, capital, (information) technology and resources. _____ became part of the business lexicon during the 1980s.
   a. Opinion leadership
   b. Unemployment insurance
   c. Outsourcing
   d. Operant conditioning

11. _____ is the corporate management term for the act of reorganizing the legal, ownership, operational, or other structures of a company for the purpose of making it more profitable, or better organized for its present needs. Alternate reasons for _____ include a change of ownership or ownership structure, demerger repositioning debt _____ and financial _____.
   a. Market value added
   b. Restructuring
   c. Market value
   d. Net worth

12. _____ is, in very basic words, a position a firm occupies against its competitors.

According to Michael Porter, the three methods for creating a sustainable _____ are through:

1. Cost leadership

2. Differentiation

3. Focus (economics)

   a. Theory Z
   b. 28-hour day
   c. 1990 Clean Air Act
   d. Competitive advantage

13. _____ is the process by which an organization deals with any major unpredictable event that threatens to harm the organization, its stakeholders, or the general public. Three elements are common to most definitions of crisis: (a) a threat to the organization, (b) the element of surprise, and (c) a short decision time.

Whereas risk management involves assessing potential threats and finding the best ways to avoid those threats, _____ involves dealing with the disasters after they have occurred.

a. Capability management
b. Business value
c. C-A-K-E
d. Crisis management

Chapter 2. The Evolution of Management Thought

1. _____ or lean production, which is often known simply as 'Lean', is a production practice that considers the expenditure of resources for any goal other than the creation of value for the end customer to be wasteful, and thus a target for elimination. Working from the perspective of the customer who consumes a product or service, 'value' is defined as any action or process that a customer would be willing to pay for. Basically, lean is centered around creating more value with less work.
   a. Six Sigma
   b. Theory of constraints
   c. Lean manufacturing
   d. Production line

2. _____ is a theory of management that analyzes and synthesizes workflows, with the objective of improving labour productivity. The core ideas of the theory were developed by Frederick Winslow Taylor in the 1880s and 1890s, and were first published in his monographs, Shop Management and The Principles of _____ Taylor believed that decisions based upon tradition and rules of thumb should be replaced by precise procedures developed after careful study of an individual at work.
   a. Capacity planning
   b. Scientific management
   c. Master production schedule
   d. Value engineering

3. The _____ is a monograph published by Frederick Winslow Taylor in 1911. This influential monograph is the basis of modern organization and decision theory and has motivated administrators and students of managerial technique. Taylor was an American mechanical engineer and a management consultant in his later years.
   a. 33 Strategies of War
   b. 28-hour day
   c. 1990 Clean Air Act
   d. Principles of Scientific Management

4. A _____ is a set of instructions having the force of a directive, covering those features of operations that lend themselves to a definite or standardized procedure without loss of effectiveness. Standard Operating Policies and Procedures can be effective catalysts to drive performance improvement and improving organizational results.
   a. 1990 Clean Air Act
   b. Standard operating procedure
   c. Risk-benefit analysis
   d. Longitudinal study

5. _____ is the process by which the activities of an organisation, particularly those regarding decision-making, become concentrated within a particular location and/or group.

a. Chief operating officer
b. Product innovation
c. Centralization
d. Corner office

6. The _____ is a standardized, on-scene, all-hazard incident management concept. It is a management protocol originally designed for emergency management agencies in the United States which was later federalized there. It has since been adopted by agencies in other countries.

a. AAAI
b. A Stake in the Outcome
c. A4e
d. Incident Command Structure

7. _____ is an organization's process of defining its strategy and making decisions on allocating its resources to pursue this strategy, including its capital and people. Various business analysis techniques can be used in _____, including SWOT analysis (Strengths, Weaknesses, Opportunities, and Threats) and PEST analysis (Political, Economic, Social, and Technological analysis) or STEER analysis involving Socio-cultural, Technological, Economic, Ecological, and Regulatory factors and EPISTEL (Environment, Political, Informatic, Social, Technological, Economic and Legal)

_____ is the formal consideration of an organization's future course. All _____ deals with at least one of three key questions:

1. 'What do we do?'
2. 'For whom do we do it?'
3. 'How do we excel?'

In business _____, the third question is better phrased 'How can we beat or avoid competition?'. (Bradford and Duncan, page 1.)

a. 33 Strategies of War
b. 1990 Clean Air Act
c. 28-hour day
d. Strategic planning

8. The _____ is a form of reactivity whereby subjects improve an aspect of their behavior being experimentally measured simply in response to the fact that they are being studied, not in response to any particular experimental manipulation.

The term was coined in 1955 by Henry A. Landsberger when analyzing older experiments from 1924-1932 at the Hawthorne Works (outside Chicago.) Hawthorne Works had commissioned a study to see if its workers would become more productive in higher or lower levels of light.

   a. 33 Strategies of War
   b. 1990 Clean Air Act
   c. 28-hour day
   d. Hawthorne effect

9. The _____ is the interlocking social structure that governs how people work together in practice. It is the aggregate of behaviors, interactions, norms, personal and professional connections through which work gets done and relationships are built among people who share a common organizational affiliation or cluster of affiliations. It consists of a dynamic set of personal relationships, social networks, communities of common interest, and emotional sources of motivation. The _____ evolves organically and spontaneously in response to changes in the work environment, the flux of people through its porous boundaries, and the complex social dynamics of its members.

   a. Informal organization
   b. Union shop
   c. Open shop
   d. Organizational effectiveness

10. _____ Movement refers to those researchers of organizational development who study the behavior of people in groups, in particular workplace groups. It originated in the 1920s' Hawthorne studies, which examined the effects of social relations, motivation and employee satisfaction on factory productivity. The movement viewed workers in terms of their psychology and fit with companies, rather than as interchangeable parts.

   a. Work design
   b. Human relations
   c. Participatory management
   d. Hersey-Blanchard situational theory

11. _____ refers to those researchers of organizational development who study the behavior of people in groups, in particular workplace groups. It originated in the 1920s' Hawthorne studies, which examined the effects of social relations, motivation and employee satisfaction on factory productivity. The movement viewed workers in terms of their psychology and fit with companies, rather than as interchangeable parts.

   a. Job analysis
   b. Job satisfaction
   c. Path-goal theory
   d. Human relations movement

12. _____ and Theory Y are theories of human motivation created and developed by Douglas McGregor at the MIT Sloan School of Management in the 1960s that have been used in human resource management, organizational behavior, organizational communication and organizational development. They describe two very different attitudes toward workforce motivation. McGregor felt that companies followed either one or the other approach.

In _____, which many managers practice, management assumes employees are inherently lazy and will avoid work if they can. They inherently dislike work. Because of this, workers need to be closely supervised and comprehensive systems of controls developed.

   a. Theory X
   b. Management team
   c. Cash cow
   d. Job enrichment

13. Theory X and _____ are theories of human motivation created and developed by Douglas McGregor at the MIT Sloan School of Management in the 1960s that have been used in human resource management, organizational behavior, organizational communication and organizational development. They describe two very different attitudes toward workforce motivation. McGregor felt that companies followed either one or the other approach.

In _____, management assumes employees may be ambitious and self-motivated and exercise self-control. It is believed that employees enjoy their mental and physical work duties.

   a. Design leadership
   b. Contingency theory
   c. Business Workflow Analysis
   d. Theory Y

14. A _____ is a subset of the overall internal controls of a business covering the application of people, documents, technologies, and procedures by management accountants to solving business problems such as costing a product, service or a business-wide strategy. _____s are distinct from regular information systems in that they are used to analyze other information systems applied in operational activities in the organization. Academically, the term is commonly used to refer to the group of information management methods tied to the automation or support of human decision making, e.g. Decision Support Systems, Expert systems, and Executive information systems.

   a. Strategic information system
   b. 1990 Clean Air Act
   c. 28-hour day
   d. Management information system

Chapter 2. The Evolution of Management Thought

15. _____, is the discipline of using scientific research-based principles, strategies, and other analytical methods, such as mathematical modeling to improve any organization's ability to enact rational, meaningful business management decisions.
    a. Management science
    b. Trustee
    c. Cross ownership
    d. Workflow

16. _____ is an area of business concerned with the production of goods and services, and involves the responsibility of ensuring that business operations are efficient in terms of using as little resource as needed, and effective in terms of meeting customer requirements. It is concerned with managing the process that converts inputs (in the forms of materials, labour and energy) into outputs (in the form of goods and services.)

    Operations traditionally refers to the production of goods and services separately, although the distinction between these two main types of operations is increasingly difficult to make as manufacturers tend to merge product and service offerings.

    a. AAAI
    b. Operations management
    c. A Stake in the Outcome
    d. A4e

17. _____ is a business management strategy aimed at embedding awareness of quality in all organizational processes. _____ has been widely used in manufacturing, education, hospitals, call centers, government, and service industries, as well as NASA space and science programs.

    As defined by the International Organization for Standardization (ISO):

    '_____ is a management approach for an organization, centered on quality, based on the participation of all its members and aiming at long-term success through customer satisfaction, and benefits to all members of the organization and to society.' ISO 8402:1994

    One major aim is to reduce variation from every process so that greater consistency of effort is obtained. (Royse, D., Thyer, B., Padgett D., ' Logan T., 2006)

    a. Quality management
    b. 1990 Clean Air Act
    c. 28-hour day
    d. Total quality management

18. _____ can be considered to have three main components: quality control, quality assurance and quality improvement. _____ is focused not only on product quality, but also the means to achieve it. _____ therefore uses quality assurance and control of processes as well as products to achieve more consistent quality.
   a. Quality management
   b. Total quality management
   c. 28-hour day
   d. 1990 Clean Air Act

19. _____ is a class of behavioural theory that claims that there is no best way to organize a corporation, to lead a company, or to make decisions. Instead, the optimal course of action is contingent (dependant) upon the internal and external situation. Several contingency approaches were developed concurrently in the late 1960s.
   a. Capability management
   b. Contingency theory
   c. Commercial management
   d. Distributed management

20. _____ is the term used to describe a situation where different entities cooperate advantageously for a final outcome. Simply defined, it means that the whole is greater than the sum of the individual parts. Although the whole will be greater than each individual part, this is not the concept of _____.
   a. Synergy
   b. 33 Strategies of War
   c. 1990 Clean Air Act
   d. 28-hour day

Chapter 3. Values, Attitudes, Emotions, and Culture: The Manager as a Person

1. In psychology, _____ is a major approach to the study of human personality. Trait theorists are primarily interested in the measurement of traits, which can be defined as habitual patterns of behavior, thought, and emotion. According to this perspective, traits are relatively stable over time, differ among individuals (e.g. some people are outgoing whereas others are shy), and influence behavior.
    a. Psychological statistics
    b. Trait theory
    c. Cognitive dissonance
    d. Psychometrics

2. Negative Affect is a general dimension of subjective distress and unpleasurable engagement that subsumes a variety of aversive mood states, including anger, contempt, disgust, guilt, fear, and nervousness. Individuals high in _____ are characterized by distress, un-pleasurable engagement, and nervousness. Low negative affect is characterised by a state of calmness and serenity.
    a. 33 Strategies of War
    b. Negative affectivity
    c. 1990 Clean Air Act
    d. 28-hour day

3. _____ is one of five major domains of personality discovered by psychologists. Openness involves active imagination, aesthetic sensitivity, attentiveness to inner feelings, preference for variety, and intellectual curiosity. A great deal of psychometric research has demonstrated that these qualities are statistically correlated.
    a. Openness to experience
    b. Introverts
    c. Introversion
    d. Extraversion

4. _____ is a term in psychology which refers to a person's belief about what causes the good or bad results in his or her life, either in general or in a specific area such as health or academics. Understanding of the concept was developed by Julian B. Rotter in 1954, and has since become an important aspect of personality studies.

    _____ refers to the extent to which individuals believe that they can control events that affect them.

    a. Social loafing
    b. Machiavellianism
    c. Self-enhancement
    d. Locus of control

5. In psychology, _____ reflects a person's overall evaluation or appraisal of his or her own worth.

Chapter 3. Values, Attitudes, Emotions, and Culture: The Manager as a Person   13

_____ encompasses beliefs (for example, 'I am competent/incompetent') and emotions (for example, triumph/despair, pride/shame.) Behavior may reflect _____

   a. 33 Strategies of War
   b. 28-hour day
   c. 1990 Clean Air Act
   d. Self-esteem

6. _____ is one of the managerial functions like planning, organizing, staffing and directing. It is an important function because it helps to check the errors and to take the corrective action so that deviation from standards are minimized and stated goals of the organization are achieved in desired manner. According to modern concepts, _____ is a foreseeing action whereas earlier concept of _____ was used only when errors were detected. _____ in management means setting standards, measuring actual performance and taking corrective action.
   a. Control
   b. Turnover
   c. Schedule of reinforcement
   d. Decision tree pruning

7. _____ refers to an individual's desire for significant accomplishment, mastering of skills, control, or high standards. The term was introduced by the psychologist, David McClelland.

_____ is related to the difficulty of tasks people choose to undertake.

   a. Need for power
   b. Two-factor theory
   c. 1990 Clean Air Act
   d. Need for achievement

8. The _____ is a term that was popularised by David McClelland and describes a person's need to feel a sense of involvement and 'belonging' within a social group. However, it should be recognised that McClellend's thinking was strongly influenced by the pioneering work of Henry Murray who first identified underlying psychological human needs and motivational processes (1938.) It was Murray who set out a taxonomy of needs, including Achievement, Power and Affiliation - and placed these in the context of an integrated motivational model.
   a. SESAMO
   b. Need for affiliation
   c. Polynomial conjoint measurement
   d. Strong-Campbell Interest Inventory

Chapter 3. Values, Attitudes, Emotions, and Culture: The Manager as a Person

9. _____ is a term that was popularized by renowned psychologist David McClelland in 1961. However, it should be recognized that McClellend's thinking was strongly influenced by the pioneering work of Henry Murray who first identified underlying psychological human needs and motivational processes (1938.) It was Murray who set out a taxonomy of needs, including Achievement, Power and Affiliation - and placed these in the context of an integrated motivational model.
   a. Need for Achievement
   b. Two-factor theory
   c. Need for power
   d. 1990 Clean Air Act

10. In law, _____ is the term to describe a partnership between two or more parties.

In England a number of statutes on the subject have been passed, the chief being the Bastardy Act of 1845, and the Bastardy Laws Amendment Acts of 1872 and 1873. The mother of a bastard may summon the putative father to petty sessions within twelve months of the birth (or at any later time if he is proved to have contributed to the child's support within twelve months after the birth), and the justices, as after hearing evidence on both sides, may, if the mother's evidence be corroborated in some material particular, adjudge the man to be the putative father of the child, and order him to pay a sum not exceeding five shillings a week for its maintenance, together with a sum for expenses incidental to the birth, or the funeral expenses, if it has died before the date of order, and the costs of the proceedings.

   a. Abraham Harold Maslow
   b. Affiliation
   c. Adam Smith
   d. Affiliation

11. _____ is the value of objects, both physical objects and abstract objects, not as ends-in-themselves but a means of achieving something else. It is often contrasted with items of intrinsic value.

It is studied in the field of value theory.

   a. A4e
   b. A Stake in the Outcome
   c. AAAI
   d. Instrumental value

12. A _____ is a set of consistent ethic values (more specifically the personal and cultural values) and measures used for the purpose of ethical or ideological integrity. A well defined _____ is a moral code.

Fred Wenst>øp and Arild Myrmel have proposed a structure for corporate _____s that consists of three value categories. These are considered complementary and juxtaposed on the same level if illustrated graphically on for instance an organization's web page. The first value category is Core Values, which prescribe the attitude and character of an organization, and are often found in sections on Code of conduct on its web page. The philosophical antecedents of these values are Virtue ethics, which is often attributed to Aristotle. Protected Values are protected through rules, standards and certifications. They are often concerned with areas such as health, environment and safety. The third category, Created Values, is the values that stakeholders, including the shareholders expect in return for their contributions to the firm. These values are subject to trade-off by decision-makers or bargaining processes. This process is explained further in Stakeholder theory.

   a. 1990 Clean Air Act
   b. 28-hour day
   c. Value system
   d. 33 Strategies of War

13. _____ describes how content an individual is with his or her job.

The happier people are within their job, the more satisfied they are said to be. _____ is not the same as motivation, although it is clearly linked.

   a. Human relations
   b. Job analysis
   c. Goal-setting theory
   d. Job satisfaction

14. _____ , often measured as an _____ Quotient (EQ), is a term that describes the ability, capacity, skill or (in the case of the trait _____ model) a self-perceived ability, to identify, assess, and manage the emotions of one's self, of others, and of groups. Different models have been proposed for the definition of _____ and disagreement exists as to how the term should be used. Despite these disagreements, which are often highly technical, the ability _____ and trait _____ models (but not the mixed models) are enjoying considerable support in the literature and have successful applications in many different domains.
   a. Emotional intelligence
   b. A Stake in the Outcome
   c. AAAI
   d. A4e

Chapter 3. Values, Attitudes, Emotions, and Culture: The Manager as a Person

15. _____ is an idea in the field of Organizational studies and management which describes the psychology, attitudes, experiences, beliefs and Values (personal and cultural values) of an organization. It has been defined as 'the specific collection of values and norms that are shared by people and groups in an organization and that control the way they interact with each other and with stakeholders outside the organization.'

This definition continues to explain organizational values also known as 'beliefs and ideas about what kinds of goals members of an organization should pursue and ideas about the appropriate kinds or standards of behavior organizational members should use to achieve these goals. From organizational values develop organizational norms, guidelines or expectations that prescribe appropriate kinds of behavior by employees in particular situations and control the behavior of organizational members towards one another.'

_____ is not the same as corporate culture.

a. Organizational culture
b. Organizational development
c. Organizational effectiveness
d. Union shop

16. An _____ is a meeting that official bodies, and associations involving the public, are often required by law to hold.

An _____ is generally held every year to inform their members of previous and future activities. It is an opportunity for the shareholders and partners to receive copies of the company's accounts as well as reviewing fiscal information for the past year and asking any questions regarding the decisions the business will take in the future.

a. Annual general meeting
b. A Stake in the Outcome
c. A4e
d. AAAI

Chapter 4. Ethics and Social Responsibility

1. An _____ is a situation that will often involve an apparent conflict between moral imperatives, in which to obey one would result in transgressing another. This is also called an ethical paradox since in moral philosophy, paradox plays a central role in ethics debates. For instance, an ethical admonition to 'love thy neighbour as thy self' is not always just in contrast with, but sometimes in contradiction to an armed neighbour actively trying to kill you: if he or she succeeds, you will not be able to love him or her.
   a. A Stake in the Outcome
   b. A4e
   c. AAAI
   d. Ethical dilemma

2. A mutual shareholder or _____ is an individual or company (including a corporation) that legally owns one or more shares of stock in a joint stock company. A company's shareholders collectively own that company. Thus, the typical goal of such companies is to enhance shareholder value.
   a. 1990 Clean Air Act
   b. Shareholder
   c. Free riding
   d. Stockholder

3. _____ can be regarded as an outcome of mental processes (cognitive process) leading to the selection of a course of action among several alternatives. Every _____ process produces a final choice. The output can be an action or an opinion of choice.
   a. 28-hour day
   b. 1990 Clean Air Act
   c. Decision making
   d. 33 Strategies of War

4. The _____ of 1977 (15 U.S.C. §§ 78dd-1, et seq.) is a United States federal law known primarily for two of its main provisions, one that addresses accounting transparency requirements under the Securities Exchange Act of 1934 and another concerning bribery of foreign officials.
   a. Limited liability
   b. Foreign Corrupt Practices Act
   c. Social Security Act of 1965
   d. Meritor Savings Bank v. Vinson

5. _____ is the ethics of an organization, and it is how an organization ethically responds to an internal or external stimulus. _____ is interdependent with the organizational culture. Although, it is akin to both organizational behavior (OB) and business ethics on the micro and macro levels, _____ is neither OB, nor is it solely business ethics (which includes corporate governance and corporate ethics.)

a. Organizational ethics
b. A4e
c. AAAI
d. A Stake in the Outcome

6. _____ is an idea in the field of Organizational studies and management which describes the psychology, attitudes, experiences, beliefs and Values (personal and cultural values) of an organization. It has been defined as 'the specific collection of values and norms that are shared by people and groups in an organization and that control the way they interact with each other and with stakeholders outside the organization.'

This definition continues to explain organizational values also known as 'beliefs and ideas about what kinds of goals members of an organization should pursue and ideas about the appropriate kinds or standards of behavior organizational members should use to achieve these goals. From organizational values develop organizational norms, guidelines or expectations that prescribe appropriate kinds of behavior by employees in particular situations and control the behavior of organizational members towards one another.'

_____ is not the same as corporate culture.

a. Organizational development
b. Organizational effectiveness
c. Organizational culture
d. Union shop

Chapter 5. Managing Diverse Employees in a Multicultural Environment

1. The 'business case for _____', theorizes that in a global marketplace, a company that employs a diverse workforce (both men and women, people of many generations, people from ethnically and racially diverse backgrounds etc.) is better able to understand the demographics of the marketplace it serves and is thus better equipped to thrive in that marketplace than a company that has a more limited range of employee demographics.

An additional corollary suggests that a company that supports the _____ of its workforce can also improve employee satisfaction, productivity and retention.

   a. Trademark
   b. Kanban
   c. Virtual team
   d. Diversity

2. In economics, the term _____ refers to situations where the advancement of a qualified person within the hierarchy of an organization is stopped at a lower level because of some form of discrimination, most commonly sexism or racism, but since the term was coined, '_____' has also come to describe the limited advancement of the deaf, blind, disabled, aged and sexual minorities. It is an unofficial, invisible barrier that prevents women and minorities from advancing in businesses.

This situation is referred to as a 'ceiling' as there is a limitation blocking upward advancement, and 'glass' (transparent) because the limitation is not immediately apparent and is normally an unwritten and unofficial policy. This invisible barrier continues to exist, even though there are no explicit obstacles keeping minorities from acquiring advanced job positions - there are no advertisements that specifically say 'no minorities hired at this establishment', nor are there any formal orders that say 'minorities are not qualified' - but they do lie beneath the surface.

   a. 28-hour day
   b. 1990 Clean Air Act
   c. 33 Strategies of War
   d. Glass ceiling

3. The _____ of 1967, Pub. L. No. 90-202, 81 Stat. 602 (Dec. 15, 1967), codified as Chapter 14 of Title 29 of the United States Code, 29 U.S.C. § 621 through 29 U.S.C. § 634 (ADEA), prohibits employment discrimination against persons 40 years of age or older in the United States). The law also sets standards for pensions and benefits provided by employers and requires that information about the needs of older workers be provided to the general public.
   a. Unemployment and Farm Relief Act
   b. Undue hardship
   c. Age Discrimination in Employment Act
   d. Extra time

Chapter 5. Managing Diverse Employees in a Multicultural Environment

4. The _____ of 1990 (ADA) is the short title of United States (Pub.L. 101-336, 104 Stat. 327, enacted July 26, 1990), codified at 42 U.S.C. Â§ 12101 et seq. It was signed into law on July 26, 1990, by President George H. W. Bush, and later amended with changes effective January 1, 2009. The ADA is a wide-ranging civil rights law that prohibits, under certain circumstances, discrimination based on disability. It affords similar protections against discrimination to Americans with disabilities as the Civil Rights Act of 1964,
   a. Equal Pay Act of 1963
   b. Americans with Disabilities Act
   c. Employment discrimination
   d. Australian labour law

5. The _____ is a United States statute that was passed in response to a series of United States Supreme Court decisions which limited the rights of employees who had sued their employers for discrimination. The Act represented the first effort since the passage of the Civil Rights Act of 1964 to modify some of the basic procedural and substantive rights provided by federal law in employment discrimination cases. It provided for the right to trial by jury on discrimination claims and introduced the possibility of emotional distress damages, while limiting the amount that a jury could award

The 1991 Act combined elements from two different civil rights acts of the past: the Civil Rights Act of 1866, better known by the number assigned to it in the codification of federal laws as 'Section 1981', and the employment-related provisions of the Civil Rights Act of 1964, generally referred to as 'Title VII', its location within the Act.

   a. Covenant
   b. Negligence in employment
   c. Resource Conservation and Recovery Act
   d. Civil Rights Act of 1991

6. _____ is a contract between two parties, one being the employer and the other being the employee. An employee may be defined as: 'A person in the service of another under any contract of hire, express or implied, oral or written, where the employer has the power or right to control and direct the employee in the material details of how the work is to be performed.' Black's Law Dictionary page 471 (5th ed. 1979.)
   a. Exit interview
   b. Employment rate
   c. Employment
   d. Employment counsellor

7. The _____ 1970 is an Act of the United Kingdom Parliament which prohibits any less favourable treatment between men and women in terms of pay and conditions of employment. It came into force on 29 December 1975. The term pay is interpreted in a broad sense to include, on top of wages, things like holidays, pension rights, company perks and some kinds of bonuses.

Chapter 5. Managing Diverse Employees in a Multicultural Environment

a. Australian labour law
b. Equal Pay Act
c. Oncale v. Sundowner Offshore Services
d. Architectural Barriers Act of 1968

8. The term _____ was created by President Lyndon B. Johnson when he signed Executive Order 11246 on September 24, 1965, created to prohibit federal contractors from discriminating against employees on the basis of race, sex, creed, religion, color, or national origin. In more recent times, most employers have also added sexual orientation to the list of non-discrimination.

The Executive Order also required contractors to implement affirmative action plans to increase the participation of minorities and women in the workplace.

a. AAAI
b. A4e
c. A Stake in the Outcome
d. Equal employment opportunity

9. The _____ is a United States labor law allowing an employee to take unpaid leave due to a serious health condition that makes the employee unable to perform his job or to care for a sick family member or to care for a new son or daughter (including by birth, adoption or foster care.) The bill was among the first signed into law by President Bill Clinton in his first term.

a. Family and Medical Leave Act of 1993
b. Contributory negligence
c. Harvester Judgment
d. Sarbanes-Oxley Act of 2002

10. _____ occurs when expectant women are fired, not hired, or otherwise discriminated against due to their pregnancy or intention to become pregnant. Common forms of _____ include not being hired due to visible pregnancy or likelihood of becoming pregnant, being fired after informing an employer of one's pregnancy, being fired after maternity leave, and receiving a pay dock due to pregnancy. In the United States, since 1978, employers are legally bound to provide what insurance, leave pay, and additional support that would be bestowed upon any employee with medical leave or disability.

a. Pregnancy Discrimination
b. 28-hour day
c. 1990 Clean Air Act
d. 33 Strategies of War

Chapter 5. Managing Diverse Employees in a Multicultural Environment

11. An _____ is a person who has possession of an enterprise and assumes significant accountability for the inherent risks and the outcome. It is an ambitious leader who combines land, labor, and capital to create and market new goods or services. The term is a loanword from French and was first defined by the Irish economist Richard Cantillon.
    a. A Stake in the Outcome
    b. AAAI
    c. Entrepreneur
    d. A4e

12. In politics, a _____, (by metaphor with the carved _____ at the prow of a sailing ship), is a person who holds an important title or office yet executes little actual power, most commonly limited by convention rather than law. Common _____s include constitutional monarchs, such as: Queen Elizabeth II, the Emperor of Japan, or presidents in parliamentary democracies, such as the President of Israel.

    While the authority of a _____ is in practice generally symbolic, public opinion, respect for the office or the office holder and access to high levels of government can give them significant influence on events.

    a. 1990 Clean Air Act
    b. 28-hour day
    c. Figurehead
    d. 33 Strategies of War

13. There are two types of _____ relationships: formal and informal. Informal relationships develop on their own between partners. Formal _____, on the other hand, refers to assigned relationships, often associated with organizational _____ programs designed to promote employee development or to assist at-risk children and youth.
    a. Real Property Administrator
    b. Human resource management system
    c. Fix it twice
    d. Mentoring

14. A _____ exists when an employee experiences workplace harassment and fears going to work because of the offensive, intimidating religion, sex, national origin, age, disability, veteran status, or, in some jurisdictions, sexual orientation, political affiliation, citizenship status, marital status, or personal appearance. _____ is also one of the two legal categories of sexual harassment.

    The anti-discrimination statutes governing _____ are not a general civility code.

Chapter 5. Managing Diverse Employees in a Multicultural Environment

a. Contrat nouvelle embauche
b. Flextime
c. Financial Security Law of France
d. Hostile work environment

15. _____ indicates a more-or-less equal exchange or substitution of goods or services. English speakers often use the term to mean 'a favour for a favour' and the phrases with almost identical meaning include: 'what for what,' 'give and take,' 'tit for tat', 'this for that', and 'you scratch my back, and I'll scratch yours'.

In legal usage, _____ indicates that an item or a service has been traded in return for something of value, usually when the propriety or equity of the transaction is in question.

a. 1990 Clean Air Act
b. Quid pro quo
c. 33 Strategies of War
d. 28-hour day

16. _____ is unwelcome harassment of a sexual nature, or based upon the receiving party's sex or gender. In some contexts or circumstances, _____ may be illegal. It includes a range of behavior from seemingly mild transgressions and annoyances to actual sexual abuse or sexual assault.

a. Hypernorms
b. 28-hour day
c. 1990 Clean Air Act
d. Sexual harassment

Chapter 6. Managing in the Global Environment

1. _____ is subcontracting a process, such as product design or manufacturing, to a third-party company. The decision to outsource is often made in the interest of lowering cost or making better use of time and energy costs, redirecting or conserving energy directed at the competencies of a particular business, or to make more efficient use of land, labor, capital, (information) technology and resources. _____ became part of the business lexicon during the 1980s.
   a. Opinion leadership
   b. Outsourcing
   c. Operant conditioning
   d. Unemployment insurance

2. A _____ is the system of organizations, people, technology, activities, information and resources involved in moving a product or service from supplier to customer. _____ activities transform natural resources, raw materials and components into a finished product that is delivered to the end customer. In sophisticated _____ systems, used products may re-enter the _____ at any point where residual value is recyclable.
   a. Packaging
   b. Drop shipping
   c. Wholesalers
   d. Supply chain

3. _____ is the management of a network of interconnected businesses involved in the ultimate provision of product and service packages required by end customers (Harland, 1996.) _____ spans all movement and storage of raw materials, work-in-process inventory, and finished goods from point of origin to point of consumption (supply chain.)

   The definition an American professional association put forward is that _____ encompasses the planning and management of all activities involved in sourcing, procurement, conversion, and logistics management activities.

   a. Supply chain management
   b. Packaging
   c. Drop shipping
   d. Freight forwarder

4. In economics and especially in the theory of competition, _____ are obstacles in the path of a firm that make it difficult to enter a given market.

   _____ are the source of a firm's pricing power - the ability of a firm to raise prices without losing all its customers.

   The term refers to hindrances that an individual may face while trying to gain entrance into a profession or trade.

a. 28-hour day
b. Barriers to entry
c. Predatory pricing
d. 1990 Clean Air Act

5. A _____ is a name or trademark connected with a product or producer. _____s have become increasingly important components of culture and the economy, now being described as 'cultural accessories and personal philosophies'.

Some people distinguish the psychological aspect of a _____ from the experiential aspect.

a. Brand loyalty
b. Brand awareness
c. Brand extension
d. Brand

6. _____, in marketing, consists of a consumer's commitment to repurchase or otherwise continue using the brand and can be demonstrated by repeated buying of a product or service or other positive behaviors such as word of mouth advocacy.

_____ is more than simple repurchasing, however. Customers may repurchase a brand due to situational constraints, a lack of viable alternatives, or out of convenience.

a. Brand loyalty
b. Brand awareness
c. Brand extension
d. Brand image

7. _____, in microeconomics, are the cost advantages that a business obtains due to expansion. They are factors that cause a producer's average cost per unit to fall as scale is increased. _____ is a long run concept and refers to reductions in unit cost as the size of a facility, or scale, increases.

a. Economies of scope
b. A Stake in the Outcome
c. A4e
d. Economies of scale

Chapter 6. Managing in the Global Environment

8. _____ or _____ data refers to selected population characteristics as used in government, marketing or opinion research, or the _____ profiles used in such research. Note the distinction from the term 'demography' Commonly-used _____s include race, age, income, disabilities, mobility (in terms of travel time to work or number of vehicles available), educational attainment, home ownership, employment status, and even location.
   a. Abraham Harold Maslow
   b. Demographic
   c. Affiliation
   d. Adam Smith

9. _____ in its literal sense is the process of transformation of local or regional phenomena into global ones. It can be described as a process by which the people of the world are unified into a single society and function together.

This process is a combination of economic, technological, sociocultural and political forces.

   a. Cost Management
   b. Collaborative Planning, Forecasting and Replenishment
   c. Histogram
   d. Globalization

10. The _____ was the outcome of the failure of negotiating governments to create the International Trade Organization (ITO.) GATT was formed in 1947 and lasted until 1994, when it was replaced by the World Trade Organization. The Bretton Woods Conference had introduced the idea for an organization to regulate trade as part of a larger plan for economic recovery after World War II.
   a. 1990 Clean Air Act
   b. Multilateral treaty
   c. General Agreement on Tariffs and Trade
   d. 28-hour day

11. _____ is a type of trade policy that allows traders to act and transact without interference from government. Thus, the policy permits trading partners mutual gains from trade, with goods and services produced according to the theory of comparative advantage.

Under a _____ policy, prices are a reflection of true supply and demand, and are the sole determinant of resource allocation.

a. 33 Strategies of War
b. Free trade
c. 28-hour day
d. 1990 Clean Air Act

12. The _____ is a trilateral trade bloc in North America created by the governments of the United States, Canada, and Mexico. The agreement creating the trade bloc came into force on January 1, 1994. It superseded the Canada-United States Free Trade Agreement between the U.S. and Canada.
    a. Career portfolios
    b. Trade union
    c. Business war game
    d. North American Free Trade Agreement

13. _____ is a term used to describe any moral, political that stresses human interdependence and the importance of a collective, rather than the importance of separate individuals. Collectivists focus on community and society, and seek to give priority to group goals over individual goals. The philosophical underpinnings of _____ are for some related to holism or organicism - the view that the whole is greater than the sum of its parts/pieces.
    a. Collaborative methods
    b. 1990 Clean Air Act
    c. 28-hour day
    d. Collectivism

Chapter 7. Decision Making, Learning, Creativity, and Entrepreneurship

1. _____ can be regarded as an outcome of mental processes (cognitive process) leading to the selection of a course of action among several alternatives. Every _____ process produces a final choice. The output can be an action or an opinion of choice.
   a. Decision making
   b. 33 Strategies of War
   c. 28-hour day
   d. 1990 Clean Air Act

2. _____ is a concept based on the fact that rationality of individuals is limited by the information they have, the cognitive limitations of their minds, and the finite amount of time they have to make decisions. This contrasts with the concept of rationality as optimization. Another way to look at _____ is that, because decision-makers lack the ability and resources to arrive at the optimal solution, they instead apply their rationality only after having greatly simplified the choices available.
   a. Complete information
   b. Transferable utility
   c. Bounded rationality
   d. Mixed strategy

3. In decision theory and estimation theory, the _____ of an estimator, $\hat{\theta}$, of an unknown parameter of the distribution, θ, is the expected value of the loss function

$$R(\theta, \hat{\theta}) = \mathbb{E}_\theta L(\theta, \hat{\theta}) = \int L(\theta, \hat{\theta})\, dP_\theta.$$

Chapter 7. Decision Making, Learning, Creativity, and Entrepreneurship

where dP_θ is a probability measure parametrized by θ.

- For a scalar parameter θ and a quadratic loss function,

$$L(\theta, \hat{\theta}) = (\theta - \hat{\theta})^2$$

the _____ function becomes the mean squared error of the estimate,

$$R(\theta, \hat{\theta}) = E_\theta (\theta - \hat{\theta})^2$$

- In density estimation, the unknown parameter is probability density itself. The loss function is typically chosen to be a norm in an appropriate function space. For example, for L^2 norm,

$$L(f, \hat{f}) = \|f - \hat{f}\|_2^2$$

the _____ function becomes the mean integrated squared error

$$R(f, \hat{f}) = E\|f - \hat{f}\|^2$$

a. Risk aversion
b. Linear model
c. Financial modeling
d. Risk

4. _____ is an adjective for experience-based techniques that help in problem solving, learning and discovery. A _____ method is particularly used to rapidly come to a solution that is hoped to be close to the best possible answer, or 'optimal solution'. _____s are 'rules of thumb', educated guesses, intuitive judgments or simply common sense.
   a. Representativeness
   b. 1990 Clean Air Act
   c. 28-hour day
   d. Heuristic

5. The _____ heuristic is a heuristic wherein people assume commonality between objects of similar appearance, or between an object and a group it appears to fit into. While often very useful in everyday life, it can also result in neglect of relevant base rates and other cognitive biases. The representative heuristic was first proposed by Amos Tversky and Daniel Kahneman.

Chapter 7. Decision Making, Learning, Creativity, and Entrepreneurship

a. Representativeness heuristic
b. Representativeness
c. 1990 Clean Air Act
d. 28-hour day

6. _____ is one of the managerial functions like planning, organizing, staffing and directing. It is an important function because it helps to check the errors and to take the corrective action so that deviation from standards are minimized and stated goals of the organization are achieved in desired manner. According to modern concepts, _____ is a foreseeing action whereas earlier concept of _____ was used only when errors were detected. _____ in management means setting standards, measuring actual performance and taking corrective action.
   a. Turnover
   b. Schedule of reinforcement
   c. Decision tree pruning
   d. Control

7. _____ is decision making in groups consisting of multiple members/entities. The challenge of group decision is deciding what action a group should take. There are various systems designed to solve this problem.
   a. Control of Substances Hazardous to Health Regulations 2002
   b. Genbutsu
   c. Collaborative Planning, Forecasting and Replenishment
   d. Groups decision making

8. _____ is a type of thought exhibited by group members who try to minimize conflict and reach consensus without critically testing, analyzing, and evaluating ideas. Individual creativity, uniqueness, and independent thinking are lost in the pursuit of group cohesiveness, as are the advantages of reasonable balance in choice and thought that might normally be obtained by making decisions as a group. During _____, members of the group avoid promoting viewpoints outside the comfort zone of consensus thinking.
   a. Psychological statistics
   b. Diffusion of responsibility
   c. Self-report inventory
   d. Groupthink

9. _____ is the pursuit of influencing outcomes -- including public-policy and resource allocation decisions within political, economic, and social systems and institutions -- that directly affect people's current lives. (Cohen, 2001)

Therefore, _____ can be seen as a deliberate process of speaking out on issues of concern in order to exert some influence on behalf of ideas or persons. Based on this definition, Cohen (2001) states that 'ideologues of all persuasions advocate' to bring a change in people's lives.

a. A4e
b. A Stake in the Outcome
c. AAAI
d. Advocacy

10. A _____ is the term given to a company that facilitates the learning of its members and continuously transforms itself. _____s develop as a result of the pressures facing modern organizations and enables them to remain competitive in the business environment. A _____ has five main features; systems thinking, personal mastery, mental models, shared vision and team learning.
   a. Hoshin Kanri
   b. 1990 Clean Air Act
   c. Quality function deployment
   d. Learning organization

11. _____ is an area of knowledge within organizational theory that studies models and theories about the way an organization learns and adapts.

In Organizational development (OD), learning is a characteristic of an adaptive organization, i.e., an organization that is able to sense changes in signals from its environment (both internal and external) and adapt accordingly.

   a. A4e
   b. A Stake in the Outcome
   c. AAAI
   d. Organizational learning

12. _____ is a group creativity technique designed to generate a large number of ideas for the solution of a problem. The method was first popularized in the late 1930s by Alex Faickney Osborn in a book called Applied Imagination. Osborn proposed that groups could double their creative output with _____.
   a. Adam Smith
   b. Abraham Harold Maslow
   c. Affiliation
   d. Brainstorming

13. The _____ is a decision making method for use among groups of many sizes, who want to make their decision quickly, as by a vote, but want everyone's opinions taken into account (as opposed to traditional voting, where only the largest group is considered). The method of tallying is the difference. First, every member of the group gives their view of the solution, with a short explanation.

Chapter 7. Decision Making, Learning, Creativity, and Entrepreneurship

a. Belief decision matrix
b. Hierarchical Decision Process
c. Decision model
d. Nominal group technique

14. The _____ is a systematic, interactive forecasting method which relies on a panel of independent experts. The carefully selected experts answer questionnaires in two or more rounds. After each round, a facilitator provides an anonymous summary of the experts' forecasts from the previous round as well as the reasons they provided for their judgments.
a. Delphi method
b. Learning organization
c. Hoshin Kanri
d. Quality function deployment

15. An _____ is a person who has possession of an enterprise and assumes significant accountability for the inherent risks and the outcome. It is an ambitious leader who combines land, labor, and capital to create and market new goods or services. The term is a loanword from French and was first defined by the Irish economist Richard Cantillon.
a. A Stake in the Outcome
b. AAAI
c. Entrepreneur
d. A4e

16. _____ according to Onuoha (2007) is the practice of starting new organizations or revitalizing mature organizations, particularly new businesses generally in response to identified opportunities. _____ is often a difficult undertaking, as a vast majority of new businesses fail. Entrepreneurial activities are substantially different depending on the type of organization that is being started.
a. A Stake in the Outcome
b. Entrepreneurship
c. AAAI
d. A4e

17. _____ is the practice of using entrepreneurial skills without taking on the risks or accountability associated with entrepreneurial activities. It is practiced by employees within an established organization using a business model. Employees, perhaps engaged in a special project within a larger firm are supposed to behave as entrepreneurs, even though they have the resources and capabilities of the larger firm to draw upon.

a. A4e
b. A Stake in the Outcome
c. AAAI
d. Intrapreneurship

Chapter 8. The Manager as a Planner and Strategist

1. A _____ is a brief written statement of the purpose of a company or organization. Ideally, a _____ guides the actions of the organization, spells out its overall goal, provides a sense of direction, and guides decision making for all levels of management.

   _____s often contain the following:

   - Purpose and aim of the organization
   - The organization's primary stakeholders: clients, stockholders, etc.
   - Responsibilities of the organization toward these stakeholders
   - Products and services offered

   In developing a _____:

   - Encourage as much input as feasible from employees, volunteers, and other stakeholders
   - Publicize it broadly

   The _____ can be used to resolve differences between business stakeholders. Stakeholders include: employees including managers and executives, stockholders, board of directors, customers, suppliers, distributors, creditors, governments (local, state, federal, etc.), unions, competitors, NGO's, and the general public.

   a. Mission statement
   b. 28-hour day
   c. 1990 Clean Air Act
   d. 33 Strategies of War

2. Organizational culture is not the same as _____. It is wider and deeper concepts, something that an organization 'is' rather than what it 'has' (according to Buchanan and Huczynski.)

   _____ is the total sum of the values, customs, traditions and meanings that make a company unique.

   a. Job analysis
   b. Path-goal theory
   c. Work design
   d. Corporate culture

3. _____ is a strategic planning method that some organizations use to make flexible long-term plans. It is in large part an adaptation and generalization of classic methods used by military intelligence.

The original method was that a group of analysts would generate simulation games for policy makers. In business applications, the emphasis on gaming the behavior of opponents was reduced (shifting more toward a game against nature). At Royal Dutch/Shell for example, _____ was viewed as changing mindsets about the exogenous part of the world, prior to formulating specific strategies.

a. Labour productivity
b. Time and attendance
c. Scenario planning
d. Retroactive overtime

4. _____ has been described as the 'process of social influence in which one person can enlist the aid and support of others in the accomplishment of a common task'. A definition more inclusive of followers comes from Alan Keith of Genentech who said '_____ is ultimately about creating a way for people to contribute to making something extraordinary happen.'

_____ is one of the most salient aspects of the organizational context. However, defining _____ has been challenging.

a. 28-hour day
b. Situational leadership
c. Leadership
d. 1990 Clean Air Act

5. _____ is a strategic planning method used to evaluate the Strengths, Weaknesses, Opportunities, and Threats involved in a project or in a business venture. It involves specifying the objective of the business venture or project and identifying the internal and external factors that are favorable and unfavorable to achieving that objective. The technique is credited to Albert Humphrey, who led a convention at Stanford University in the 1960s and 1970s using data from Fortune 500 companies.
a. Market share
b. Corporate image
c. Marketing
d. SWOT analysis

6. Often a characteristic of new markets and industries, _____ occurs when technologies or offerings are so new that standards and rules are in flux, resulting in competitive advantages that cannot be sustained. In response, companies must constantly compete in price or quality, or innovate in supply chain management, new value creation, or have enough financial capital to outlast other competitors.

Chapter 8. The Manager as a Planner and Strategist

a. Dominant Design
b. NAIRU
c. Hypercompetition
d. Learning-by-doing

7. In microeconomics and management, the term _____ describes a style of management control. Vertically integrated companies are united through a hierarchy with a common owner. Usually each member of the hierarchy produces a different product or (market-specific) service, and the products combine to satisfy a common need.

a. 1990 Clean Air Act
b. 28-hour day
c. 33 Strategies of War
d. Vertical integration

8. _____ is the term used to describe a situation where different entities cooperate advantageously for a final outcome. Simply defined, it means that the whole is greater than the sum of the individual parts. Although the whole will be greater than each individual part, this is not the concept of _____.

a. 28-hour day
b. 33 Strategies of War
c. 1990 Clean Air Act
d. Synergy

9. _____ as defined in business terms is an organization's strategic guide to globalization. A sound _____ should address these questions: what must be (versus what is) the extent of market presence in the world's major markets? How to build the necessary global presence? What must be (versus what is) the optimal locations around the world for the various value chain activities? How to run global presence into global competitive advantage?

Academic research on _____ came of age during the 1980s, including work by Michael Porter and Christopher Bartlett ' Sumantra Ghoshal. Among the forces perceived to bring about the globalization of competition were convergence in economic systems and technological change, especially in information technology, that facilitated and required the coordination of a multinational firm's strategy on a worldwide scale.

a. 28-hour day
b. 1990 Clean Air Act
c. Global strategy
d. 33 Strategies of War

Chapter 8. The Manager as a Planner and Strategist

10. _____ is exchange of capital, goods, and services across international borders or territories. In most countries, it represents a significant share of gross domestic product (GDP.) While _____ has been present throughout much of history, its economic, social, and political importance has been on the rise in recent centuries.
   a. A4e
   b. International trade
   c. A Stake in the Outcome
   d. AAAI

11. _____ refers to the methods of practicing and using another person's business philosophy. The franchisor grants the independent operator the right to distribute its products, techniques, and trademarks for a percentage of gross monthly sales and a royalty fee. Various tangibles and intangibles such as national or international advertising, training, and other support services are commonly made available by the franchisor.
   a. 1990 Clean Air Act
   b. ServiceMaster
   c. 28-hour day
   d. Franchising

12. A _____ is an entity formed between two or more parties to undertake economic activity together. The parties agree to create a new entity by both contributing equity, and they then share in the revenues, expenses, and control of the enterprise. The venture can be for one specific project only, or a continuing business relationship such as the Fuji Xerox _____.
   a. Civil Rights Act of 1991
   b. Patent
   c. Joint venture
   d. Meritor Savings Bank v. Vinson

13. A _____ is a formal relationship between two or more parties to pursue a set of agreed upon goals or to meet a critical business need while remaining independent organizations.

Partners may provide the _____ with resources such as products, distribution channels, manufacturing capability, project funding, capital equipment, knowledge, expertise, or intellectual property. The alliance is a cooperation or collaboration which aims for a synergy where each partner hopes that the benefits from the alliance will be greater than those from individual efforts.

   a. Farmshoring
   b. Process automation
   c. Golden parachute
   d. Strategic alliance

14. An _____ is a person who has possession of an enterprise and assumes significant accountability for the inherent risks and the outcome. It is an ambitious leader who combines land, labor, and capital to create and market new goods or services. The term is a loanword from French and was first defined by the Irish economist Richard Cantillon.
   a. AAAI
   b. A4e
   c. A Stake in the Outcome
   d. Entrepreneur

15. A _____, in business matters, is an entity that is controlled by a bigger and more powerful entity. The controlled entity is called a company, corporation, or limited liability company and in some cases can be a government or state-owned enterprise, and the controlling entity is called its parent (or the parent company.) The reason for this distinction is that a lone company cannot be a _____ of any organization; only an entity representing a legal fiction as a separate entity can be a _____.
   a. 33 Strategies of War
   b. Subsidiary
   c. 1990 Clean Air Act
   d. 28-hour day

Chapter 9. Value-Chain Management: Functional Strategies for Competitive Advantage

1. The _____ is a concept from business management that was first described and popularized by Michael Porter in his 1985 best-seller, Competitive Advantage: Creating and Sustaining Superior Performance.

A _____ is a chain of activities. Products pass through all activities of the chain in order and at each activity the product gains some value. The chain of activities gives the products more added value than the sum of added values of all activities. It is important not to mix the concept of the _____ with the costs occurring throughout the activities.

   a. Value chain
   b. Market development
   c. Mass marketing
   d. Customer relationship management

2. _____ is an integrated communications-based process through which individuals and communities discover that existing and newly-identified needs and wants may be satisfied by the products and services of others.

_____ is defined by the American _____ Association as the activity, set of institutions, and processes for creating, communicating, delivering, and exchanging offerings that have value for customers, clients, partners, and society at large. The term developed from the original meaning which referred literally to going to market, as in shopping, or going to a market to buy or sell goods or services.

   a. Customer relationship management
   b. Disruptive technology
   c. Market development
   d. Marketing

3. _____ is the branch of logistics that deals with the tangible components of a supply chain. Specifically, this covers the acquisition of spare parts and replacements, quality control of purchasing and ordering such parts, and the standards involved in ordering, shipping, and warehousing the said parts.

A large component of _____ is ensuring that parts and materials used in the supply chain meet minimum requirements by performing quality assurance (QA.)

   a. Delayed differentiation
   b. Supply-Chain Operations Reference
   c. Materials management
   d. Vendor Managed Inventory

Chapter 9. Value-Chain Management: Functional Strategies for Competitive Advantage

4. In business and engineering, new _____ is the term used to describe the complete process of bringing a new product or service to market. There are two parallel paths involved in the NProduct development process: one involves the idea generation, product design, and detail engineering; the other involves market research and marketing analysis. Companies typically see new _____ as the first stage in generating and commercializing new products within the overall strategic process of product life cycle management used to maintain or grow their market share.

   a. 33 Strategies of War
   b. Product development
   c. 28-hour day
   d. 1990 Clean Air Act

5. In economics, a _____ is a function that specifies the output of a firm, an industry, or an entire economy for all combinations of inputs. A meta-_____ compares the practice of the existing entities converting inputs X into output y to determine the most efficient practice _____ of the existing entities, whether the most efficient feasible practice production or the most efficient actual practice production. In either case, the maximum output of a technologically-determined production process is a mathematical function of input factors of production.

   a. Diseconomies of scale
   b. Production function
   c. Multifactor productivity
   d. Factors of production

6. _____ is the provision of service to customers before, during and after a purchase.

According to Turban et al. (2002), '_____ is a series of activities designed to enhance the level of customer satisfaction - that is, the feeling that a product or service has met the customer expectation.'

Its importance varies by product, industry and customer; defective or broken merchandise can be exchanged, often only with a receipt and within a specified time frame.

   a. 1990 Clean Air Act
   b. 28-hour day
   c. Service rate
   d. Customer service

7. _____ is an advertisement in which a particular product specifically mentions a competitor by name for the express purpose of showing why the competitor is inferior to the product naming it.

This should not be confused with parody advertisements, where a fictional product is being advertised for the purpose of poking fun at the particular advertisement, nor should it be confused with the use of a coined brand name for the purpose of comparing the product without actually naming an actual competitor. ('Wikipedia tastes better and is less filling than the Encyclopedia Galactica.')

Chapter 9. Value-Chain Management: Functional Strategies for Competitive Advantage

In the 1980s, during what has been referred to as the cola wars, soft-drink manufacturer Pepsi ran a series of advertisements where people, caught on hidden camera, in a blind taste test, chose Pepsi over rival Coca-Cola.

a. 1990 Clean Air Act
b. Comparative advertising
c. 33 Strategies of War
d. 28-hour day

8. _____ consists of the processes a company uses to track and organize its contacts with its current and prospective customers. _____ software is used to support these processes; information about customers and customer interactions can be entered, stored and accessed by employees in different company departments. Typical _____ goals are to improve services provided to customers, and to use customer contact information for targeted marketing.
   a. Marketing plan
   b. Customer relationship management
   c. Disruptive technology
   d. Green marketing

9. Quality management can be considered to have three main components: quality control, quality assurance and _____. Quality management is focused not only on product quality, but also the means to achieve it. Quality management therefore uses quality assurance and control of processes as well as products to achieve more consistent quality.
   a. Quality management
   b. 1990 Clean Air Act
   c. 28-hour day
   d. Quality improvement

10. _____ is a business management strategy, initially implemented by Motorola, that today enjoys widespread application in many sectors of industry.

_____ seeks to improve the quality of process outputs by identifying and removing the causes of defects (errors) and variation in manufacturing and business processes. It uses a set of quality management methods, including statistical methods, and creates a special infrastructure of people within the organization ('Black Belts' etc.)

Chapter 9. Value-Chain Management: Functional Strategies for Competitive Advantage

a. Theory of constraints
b. Takt time
c. Production line
d. Six Sigma

11. _____ is a business management strategy aimed at embedding awareness of quality in all organizational processes. _____ has been widely used in manufacturing, education, hospitals, call centers, government, and service industries, as well as NASA space and science programs.

As defined by the International Organization for Standardization (ISO):

'_____ is a management approach for an organization, centered on quality, based on the participation of all its members and aiming at long-term success through customer satisfaction, and benefits to all members of the organization and to society.' ISO 8402:1994

One major aim is to reduce variation from every process so that greater consistency of effort is obtained. (Royse, D., Thyer, B., Padgett D., ' Logan T., 2006)

a. 1990 Clean Air Act
b. Total quality management
c. Quality management
d. 28-hour day

12. _____ can be considered to have three main components: quality control, quality assurance and quality improvement. _____ is focused not only on product quality, but also the means to achieve it. _____ therefore uses quality assurance and control of processes as well as products to achieve more consistent quality.

a. Total quality management
b. 1990 Clean Air Act
c. 28-hour day
d. Quality management

13. _____ is an inventory strategy that strives to improve the return on investment of a business by reducing in-process inventory and its associated carrying costs. To meet _____ objectives, the process relies on signals between different points in the process. This means the process is often driven by a series of signals, or Kanban, which tell production when to make the next part. Kanban are usually 'tickets' but can be simple visual signals, such as the presence or absence of a part on a shelf. Implemented correctly, _____ can dramatically improve a manufacturing organization's return on investment, quality, and efficiency.

Chapter 9. Value-Chain Management: Functional Strategies for Competitive Advantage

a. 33 Strategies of War
b. 1990 Clean Air Act
c. 28-hour day
d. Just-in-time

14. A _____ system is a manufacturing system in which there is some amount of flexibility that allows the system to react in the case of changes, whether predicted or unpredicted. This flexibility is generally considered to fall into two categories, which both contain numerous subcategories.

The first category, machine flexibility, covers the system's ability to be changed to produce new product types, and ability to change the order of operations executed on a part. The second category is called routing flexibility, which consists of the ability to use multiple machines to perform the same operation on a part, as well as the system's ability to absorb large-scale changes, such as in volume, capacity, or capability.

a. Jidoka
b. Homeworkers
c. Manufacturing resource planning
d. Flexible manufacturing

15. _____ is a concept related to lean and just-in-time (JIT) production. The Japanese word _____ is a common term meaning 'signboard' or 'billboard'. According to Taiichi Ohno, the man credited with developing JIT, _____ is a means through which JIT is achieved.

a. Trademark
b. Risk management
c. Kanban
d. Succession planning

16. A _____ is a subset of the overall internal controls of a business covering the application of people, documents, technologies, and procedures by management accountants to solving business problems such as costing a product, service or a business-wide strategy. _____s are distinct from regular information systems in that they are used to analyze other information systems applied in operational activities in the organization. Academically, the term is commonly used to refer to the group of information management methods tied to the automation or support of human decision making, e.g. Decision Support Systems, Expert systems, and Executive information systems.

a. 1990 Clean Air Act
b. Strategic information system
c. Management information system
d. 28-hour day

Chapter 9. Value-Chain Management: Functional Strategies for Competitive Advantage

17. The process of _____ involves the introduction of a good or service that is new or substantially improved. This includes, but is not limited to, improvements in functional characteristics, technical abilities, or ease of use.
    a. Service-profit chain
    b. Product innovation
    c. Job enlargement
    d. Letter of resignation

18. A _____ is a group of employees from various functional areas of the organization - research, engineering, marketing, finance. human resources, and operations, for example - who are all focused on a specific objective and are responsible to work as a team to improve coordination and innovation across divisions and resolve mutual problems.
    a. Graduate recruitment
    b. Goal-setting theory
    c. Cross-functional team
    d. Sociotechnical systems

19. _____ is a civil designation for persons who are incorporated in a fixed or permanent way to a society or group: regular member of the working staff, permanent staff distinguished from a supernumerary.

The term '_____' and its counterpart, 'supernumerary,' originated in Spanish and Latin American academy and government; it is now also used in countries all over the world, such as France, the U.S., England, Italy, etc.

There are _____ members of surgical organizations, of universities, of gastronomical associations, etc.

   a. Numerary
   b. Affiliation
   c. Adam Smith
   d. Abraham Harold Maslow

Chapter 10. Managing Organizational Structure and Culture

1. The goal of _____ is to create an organization which will be able to continuously create value for present and future customers, optimizing and organizing it self. Some under _____ understand building blocks which are mandatory for the growth of the organization. To design an organization means to set up a stage where the drama of life will take place.

    a. AAAI
    b. A Stake in the Outcome
    c. Organizational architecture
    d. A4e

2. An _____ is a mostly hierarchical concept of subordination of entities that collaborate and contribute to serve one common aim.

    Organizations are a variant of clustered entities. The structure of an organization is usually set up in many a styles, dependent on their objectives and ambience.

    a. Informal organization
    b. Organizational development
    c. Open shop
    d. Organizational structure

3. In organizational development (OD), _____ is the application of Socio-Technical Systems principles and techniques to the humanization of work.

    The aims of _____ to improved job satisfaction, to improved through-put, to improved quality and to reduced employee problems, e.g., grievances, absenteeism.

    Under scientific management people would be directed by reason and the problems of industrial unrest would be appropriately (i.e., scientifically) addressed.

    a. Path-goal theory
    b. Management process
    c. Graduate recruitment
    d. Work design

4. _____ means increasing the scope of a job through extending the range of its job duties and responsibilities. This contradicts the principles of specialisation and the division of labour whereby work is divided into small units, each of which is performed repetitively by an individual worker. Some motivational theories suggest that the boredom and alienation caused by the division of labour can actually cause efficiency to fall.

Chapter 10. Managing Organizational Structure and Culture

a. Centralization
b. Mock interview
c. Job enlargement
d. Delayering

5. _____ is an attempt to motivate employees by giving them the opportunity to use the range of their abilities. It is an idea that was developed by the American psychologist Frederick Herzberg in the 1950s. It can be contrasted to job enlargement which simply increases the number of tasks without changing the challenge.

a. Catfish effect
b. C-A-K-E
c. Cash cow
d. Job enrichment

6. _____ describes the situation when output from (or information about the result of) an event or phenomenon in the past will influence the same event/phenomenon in the present or future. When an event is part of a chain of cause-and-effect that forms a circuit or loop, then the event is said to 'feed back' into itself.

_____ is also a synonym for:

- _____ signal; the information about the initial event that is the basis for subsequent modification of the event.
- _____ loop; the causal path that leads from the initial generation of the _____ signal to the subsequent modification of the event.

_____ is a mechanism, process or signal that is looped back to control a system within itself. Such a loop is called a _____ loop.

a. Feedback
b. Positive feedback
c. Feedback loop
d. 1990 Clean Air Act

Chapter 10. Managing Organizational Structure and Culture

7. In economics, _____ describes the state of a market with respect to competition.

   - Perfect competition, in which the market consists of a very large number of firms producing a homogeneous product.
   - Monopolistic competition where there are a large number of independent firms which have a very small proportion of the market share.
   - Oligopoly, in which a market is dominated by a small number of firms which own more than 40% of the market share.
   - Oligopsony, a market dominated by many sellers and a few buyers.
   - Monopoly, where there is only one provider of a product or service.
   - Natural monopoly, a monopoly in which economies of scale cause efficiency to increase continuously with the size of the firm. A firm is a natural monopoly if it is able to serve the entire market demand at a lower cost than any combination of two or more smaller, more specialized firms.
   - Monopsony, when there is only one buyer in a market.

The imperfectly competitive structure is quite identical to the realistic market conditions where some monopolistic competitors, monopolists, oligopolists, and duopolists exist and dominate the market conditions. The elements of _____ include the number and size distribution of firms, entry conditions, and the extent of differentiation.

These somewhat abstract concerns tend to determine some but not all details of a specific concrete market system where buyers and sellers actually meet and commit to trade.

   a. Deflation
   b. Market structure
   c. Productivity management
   d. Leading indicator

8. A _____ is a group of employees from various functional areas of the organization - research, engineering, marketing, finance. human resources, and operations, for example - who are all focused on a specific objective and are responsible to work as a team to improve coordination and innovation across divisions and resolve mutual problems.
   a. Goal-setting theory
   b. Graduate recruitment
   c. Sociotechnical systems
   d. Cross-functional team

Chapter 10. Managing Organizational Structure and Culture

9. _____ is an increasingly broadening term with which an organization, or other human system describes the combination of traditionally administrative personnel functions with acquisition and application of skills, knowledge and experience, Employee Relations and resource planning at various levels. The field draws upon concepts developed in Industrial/Organizational Psychology and System Theory. _____ has at least two related interpretations depending on context. The original usage derives from political economy and economics, where it was traditionally called labor, one of four factors of production although this perspective is changing as a function of new and ongoing research into more strategic approaches at national levels. This first usage is used more in terms of '_____ development', and can go beyond just organizations to the level of nations. The more traditional usage within corporations and businesses refers to the individuals within a firm or agency, and to the portion of the organization that deals with hiring, firing, training, and other personnel issues, typically referred to as '_____ management'.
   a. Human resources
   b. Progressive discipline
   c. Human resource management
   d. Bradford Factor

10. In a military context, the _____ is the line of authority and responsibility along which orders are passed within a military unit and between different units. The term is also used in a civilian management context describing comparable hierarchical structures of authority.
    a. French leave
    b. 1990 Clean Air Act
    c. 28-hour day
    d. Chain of command

11. _____ is a term originating in military organization theory, but now used more commonly in business management, particularly human resource management. _____ refers to the number of subordinates a supervisor has.

    In the hierarchical business organization of the past it was not uncommon to see average spans of 1 to 10 or even less. That is, one manager supervised ten employees on average.

    a. CIFMS
    b. Mentoring
    c. Senior management
    d. Span of control

12. _____ is one of the managerial functions like planning, organizing, staffing and directing. It is an important function because it helps to check the errors and to take the corrective action so that deviation from standards are minimized and stated goals of the organization are achieved in desired manner. According to modern concepts, _____ is a foreseeing action whereas earlier concept of _____ was used only when errors were detected. _____ in management means setting standards, measuring actual performance and taking corrective action.

a. Turnover
b. Decision tree pruning
c. Schedule of reinforcement
d. Control

13. _____(known as horizontal organization) refers to an organizational structure with few or no levels of intervening management between staff and managers. The idea is that well-trained workers will be more productive when they are more directly involved in the decision making process, rather than closely supervised by many layers of management.

This structure is generally possible only in smaller organizations or individual units within larger organizations.

a. 1990 Clean Air Act
b. Flat organization
c. 33 Strategies of War
d. 28-hour day

14. _____ is the process by which the activities of an organisation, particularly those regarding decision-making, become concentrated within a particular location and/or group.

a. Chief operating officer
b. Corner office
c. Product innovation
d. Centralization

15. _____ is a 'policy by which management devotes its time to investigating only those situations in which actual results differ significantly from planned results. The idea is that management should spend its valuable time concentrating on the more important items (such as shaping the company's future strategic course.) Attention is given only to material deviations requiring investigation.'

It is not entirely synonymous with the concept of exception management in that it describes a policy where absolute focus is on exception management, in contrast to moderate application of exception management.

a. C-A-K-E
b. Management by exception
c. Trustee
d. Business philosophy

Chapter 10. Managing Organizational Structure and Culture

16. _____ is an idea in the field of Organizational studies and management which describes the psychology, attitudes, experiences, beliefs and Values (personal and cultural values) of an organization. It has been defined as 'the specific collection of values and norms that are shared by people and groups in an organization and that control the way they interact with each other and with stakeholders outside the organization.'

This definition continues to explain organizational values also known as 'beliefs and ideas about what kinds of goals members of an organization should pursue and ideas about the appropriate kinds or standards of behavior organizational members should use to achieve these goals. From organizational values develop organizational norms, guidelines or expectations that prescribe appropriate kinds of behavior by employees in particular situations and control the behavior of organizational members towards one another.'

_____ is not the same as corporate culture.

a. Union shop
b. Organizational effectiveness
c. Organizational development
d. Organizational culture

17. _____ is a civil designation for persons who are incorporated in a fixed or permanent way to a society or group: regular member of the working staff, permanent staff distinguished from a supernumerary.

The term '_____' and its counterpart, 'supernumerary,' originated in Spanish and Latin American academy and government; it is now also used in countries all over the world, such as France, the U.S., England, Italy, etc.

There are _____ members of surgical organizations, of universities, of gastronomical associations, etc.

a. Adam Smith
b. Abraham Harold Maslow
c. Affiliation
d. Numerary

18. _____ is the ethics of an organization, and it is how an organization ethically responds to an internal or external stimulus. _____ is interdependent with the organizational culture. Although, it is akin to both organizational behavior (OB) and business ethics on the micro and macro levels, _____ is neither OB, nor is it solely business ethics (which includes corporate governance and corporate ethics.)

a. AAAI
b. A4e
c. A Stake in the Outcome
d. Organizational ethics

19. _____ is a contract between two parties, one being the employer and the other being the employee. An employee may be defined as: 'A person in the service of another under any contract of hire, express or implied, oral or written, where the employer has the power or right to control and direct the employee in the material details of how the work is to be performed.' Black's Law Dictionary page 471 (5th ed. 1979.)
   a. Employment rate
   b. Exit interview
   c. Employment counsellor
   d. Employment

Chapter 11. Organizational Control and Change

1. _____ is one of the managerial functions like planning, organizing, staffing and directing. It is an important function because it helps to check the errors and to take the corrective action so that deviation from standards are minimized and stated goals of the organization are achieved in desired manner. According to modern concepts, _____ is a foreseeing action whereas earlier concept of _____ was used only when errors were detected. _____ in management means setting standards, measuring actual performance and taking corrective action.

   a. Decision tree pruning
   b. Control
   c. Schedule of reinforcement
   d. Turnover

2. _____ describes the situation when output from (or information about the result of) an event or phenomenon in the past will influence the same event/phenomenon in the present or future. When an event is part of a chain of cause-and-effect that forms a circuit or loop, then the event is said to 'feed back' into itself.

   _____ is also a synonym for:

   - _____ signal; the information about the initial event that is the basis for subsequent modification of the event.
   - _____ loop; the causal path that leads from the initial generation of the _____ signal to the subsequent modification of the event.

   _____ is a mechanism, process or signal that is looped back to control a system within itself. Such a loop is called a _____ loop.

   a. Positive feedback
   b. Feedback loop
   c. 1990 Clean Air Act
   d. Feedback

3. In business, _____, operating income margin, operating profit margin or return on sales (ROS) is the ratio of operating income (operating profit in the UK) divided by net sales, usually presented in percent.

$$\text{Operating margin} = \left(\frac{\text{Operating income}}{\text{Revenue}}\right)$$

(Relevant figures in italics)

$$\text{Operating margin} = \left(\frac{6,318}{24,088}\right) = \underline{\underline{26.23\%}}$$

It is a measurement of what proportion of a company's revenue is left over, before taxes and other indirect costs (such as rent, bonus, interest, etc.), after paying for variable costs of production as wages, raw materials, etc. A good _____ is needed for a company to be able to pay for its fixed costs, such as interest on debt.

a. AAAI
b. A4e
c. Operating margin
d. A Stake in the Outcome

4. The _____ is an equation that equals the cost of goods sold divided by the average inventory. Average inventory equals beginning inventory plus ending inventory divided by 2.

The formula for _____:

The formula for average inventory:

A low turnover rate may point to overstocking, obsolescence, or deficiencies in the product line or marketing effort.

a. A4e
b. A Stake in the Outcome
c. Asset turnover
d. Inventory turnover

5. In finance, _____ is borrowing money to supplement existing funds for investment in such a way that the potential positive or negative outcome is magnified and/or enhanced. It generally refers to using borrowed funds, or debt, so as to attempt to increase the returns to equity. Deleveraging is the action of reducing borrowings.

a. Limited partners
b. Limited liability corporation
c. Gearing
d. Private equity

Chapter 11. Organizational Control and Change

6. Market _____ is a business, economics or investment term that refers to an asset's ability to be easily converted through an act of buying or selling without causing a significant movement in the price and with minimum loss of value. Money, or cash on hand, is the most liquid asset. An act of exchange of a less liquid asset with a more liquid asset is called liquidation.
    a. 28-hour day
    b. 33 Strategies of War
    c. 1990 Clean Air Act
    d. Liquidity

7. In finance, the _____ or quick ratio or liquid ratio measures the ability of a company to use its near cash or quick assets to immediately extinguish or retire its current liabilities. Quick assets include those current assets that presumably can be quickly converted to cash at close to their book values.

Generally, the acid test ratio should be 1:1 or better, however this varies widely by industry.

   a. A Stake in the Outcome
   b. Acid-test
   c. A4e
   d. Inventory turnover

8. In a human resources context, _____ or labor _____ is the rate at which an employer gains and loses employees. Simple ways to describe it are 'how long employees tend to stay' or 'the rate of traffic through the revolving door.' _____ is measured for individual companies and for their industry as a whole. If an employer is said to have a high _____ relative to its competitors, it means that employees of that company have a shorter average tenure than those of other companies in the same industry.
    a. Career portfolios
    b. Continuous
    c. Ten year occupational employment projection
    d. Turnover

9. An _____ is the annual budget of an activity stated in terms of Budget Classification Code, functional/subfunctional categories and cost accounts. It contains estimates of the total value of resources required for the performance of the operation including reimbursable work or services for others. It also includes estimates of workload in terms of total work units identified by cost accounts.

a. Inflation rate
b. Expected gain
c. Expected return
d. Operating budget

10. _____ generally refers to a list of all planned expenses and revenues. It is a plan for saving and spending. A _____ is an important concept in microeconomics, which uses a _____ line to illustrate the trade-offs between two or more goods.
   a. 1990 Clean Air Act
   b. 33 Strategies of War
   c. Budget
   d. 28-hour day

11. _____ is a process of agreeing upon objectives within an organization so that management and employees agree to the objectives and understand what they are in the organization.

The term '_____' was first popularized by Peter Drucker in his 1954 book 'The Practice of Management'.

The essence of _____ is participative goal setting, choosing course of actions and decision making.

   a. Management by objectives
   b. Clean sheet review
   c. Job enrichment
   d. Business economics

12. _____ is the process of comparing the cost, cycle time, productivity, or quality of a specific process or method to another that is widely considered to be an industry standard or best practice. Essentially, _____ provides a snapshot of the performance of your business and helps you understand where you are in relation to a particular standard. The result is often a business case for making changes in order to make improvements.
   a. Benchmarking
   b. Competitive heterogeneity
   c. Cost leadership
   d. Complementors

Chapter 12. Human Resource Management

1. _____ is the strategic and coherent approach to the management of an organisation's most valued assets - the people working there who individually and collectively contribute to the achievement of the objectives of the business. The terms '_____' and 'human resources' (HR) have largely replaced the term 'personnel management' as a description of the processes involved in managing people in organizations. In simple sense, _____ means employing people, developing their resources, utilizing, maintaining and compensating their services in tune with the job and organizational requirement.

   a. Revolving door syndrome
   b. Progressive discipline
   c. Job knowledge
   d. Human resource management

2. _____ is a business management strategy, initially implemented by Motorola, that today enjoys widespread application in many sectors of industry.

   _____ seeks to improve the quality of process outputs by identifying and removing the causes of defects (errors) and variation in manufacturing and business processes. It uses a set of quality management methods, including statistical methods, and creates a special infrastructure of people within the organization ('Black Belts' etc.)

   a. Production line
   b. Takt time
   c. Six Sigma
   d. Theory of constraints

3. The U.S. _____ is a federal agency whose goal is ending employment discrimination. The _____ investigates discrimination complaints based on an individual's race, color, national origin, religion, sex, age, disability and retaliation for reporting and/or opposing a discriminatory practice. The Commission is also tasked with filing suits on behalf of alleged victim(s) of discrimination against employers and as an adjudicatory for claims of discrimination brought against federal agencies.

   a. Airbus SAS
   b. Airbus Industrie
   c. ARCO
   d. Equal Employment Opportunity Commission

4. _____ is a contract between two parties, one being the employer and the other being the employee. An employee may be defined as: 'A person in the service of another under any contract of hire, express or implied, oral or written, where the employer has the power or right to control and direct the employee in the material details of how the work is to be performed.' Black's Law Dictionary page 471 (5th ed. 1979).

Chapter 12. Human Resource Management

a. Employment rate
b. Employment counsellor
c. Exit interview
d. Employment

5. The term _____ was created by President Lyndon B. Johnson when he signed Executive Order 11246 on September 24, 1965, created to prohibit federal contractors from discriminating against employees on the basis of race, sex, creed, religion, color, or national origin. In more recent times, most employers have also added sexual orientation to the list of non-discrimination.

The Executive Order also required contractors to implement affirmative action plans to increase the participation of minorities and women in the workplace.

a. A Stake in the Outcome
b. A4e
c. AAAI
d. Equal Employment Opportunity

6. The _____ of 1967, Pub. L. No. 90-202, 81 Stat. 602 (Dec. 15, 1967), codified as Chapter 14 of Title 29 of the United States Code, 29 U.S.C. § 621 through 29 U.S.C. § 634 (ADEA), prohibits employment discrimination against persons 40 years of age or older in the United States). The law also sets standards for pensions and benefits provided by employers and requires that information about the needs of older workers be provided to the general public.

a. Undue hardship
b. Age Discrimination in Employment Act
c. Extra time
d. Unemployment and Farm Relief Act

7. The _____ of 1990 (ADA) is the short title of United States (Pub.L. 101-336, 104 Stat. 327, enacted July 26, 1990), codified at 42 U.S.C. § 12101 et seq. It was signed into law on July 26, 1990, by President George H. W. Bush, and later amended with changes effective January 1, 2009. The ADA is a wide-ranging civil rights law that prohibits, under certain circumstances, discrimination based on disability. It affords similar protections against discrimination to Americans with disabilities as the Civil Rights Act of 1964,

a. Equal Pay Act of 1963
b. Employment discrimination
c. Australian labour law
d. Americans with Disabilities Act

8. The _____ is a United States statute that was passed in response to a series of United States Supreme Court decisions which limited the rights of employees who had sued their employers for discrimination. The Act represented the first effort since the passage of the Civil Rights Act of 1964 to modify some of the basic procedural and substantive rights provided by federal law in employment discrimination cases. It provided for the right to trial by jury on discrimination claims and introduced the possibility of emotional distress damages, while limiting the amount that a jury could award

The 1991 Act combined elements from two different civil rights acts of the past: the Civil Rights Act of 1866, better known by the number assigned to it in the codification of federal laws as 'Section 1981', and the employment-related provisions of the Civil Rights Act of 1964, generally referred to as 'Title VII', its location within the Act.

   a. Covenant
   b. Negligence in employment
   c. Resource Conservation and Recovery Act
   d. Civil Rights Act of 1991

9. The _____ 1970 is an Act of the United Kingdom Parliament which prohibits any less favourable treatment between men and women in terms of pay and conditions of employment. It came into force on 29 December 1975. The term pay is interpreted in a broad sense to include, on top of wages, things like holidays, pension rights, company perks and some kinds of bonuses.
   a. Architectural Barriers Act of 1968
   b. Equal Pay Act
   c. Australian labour law
   d. Oncale v. Sundowner Offshore Services

10. The _____ is a United States labor law allowing an employee to take unpaid leave due to a serious health condition that makes the employee unable to perform his job or to care for a sick family member or to care for a new son or daughter (including by birth, adoption or foster care.) The bill was among the first signed into law by President Bill Clinton in his first term.
    a. Sarbanes-Oxley Act of 2002
    b. Contributory negligence
    c. Harvester Judgment
    d. Family and Medical Leave Act of 1993

11. _____ occurs when expectant women are fired, not hired, or otherwise discriminated against due to their pregnancy or intention to become pregnant. Common forms of _____ include not being hired due to visible pregnancy or likelihood of becoming pregnant, being fired after informing an employer of one's pregnancy, being fired after maternity leave, and receiving a pay dock due to pregnancy. In the United States, since 1978, employers are legally bound to provide what insurance, leave pay, and additional support that would be bestowed upon any employee with medical leave or disability.

Chapter 12. Human Resource Management

a. 28-hour day
b. 33 Strategies of War
c. Pregnancy Discrimination
d. 1990 Clean Air Act

12. _____ refers to the process of screening, and selecting qualified people for a job at an organization or firm mid- and large-size organizations and companies often retain professional recruiters or outsource some of the process to _____ agencies. External _____ is the process of attracting and selecting employees from outside the organization.

The _____ industry has four main types of agencies: employment agencies, _____ websites and job search engines, 'headhunters' for executive and professional _____, and in-house _____.

a. Recruitment Process Outsourcing
b. Recruitment
c. Labour hire
d. Referral recruitment

13. In economics, _____ is the desire to own something and the ability to pay for it. The term _____ signifies the ability or the willingness to buy a particular commodity at a given point of time.

a. 33 Strategies of War
b. 28-hour day
c. 1990 Clean Air Act
d. Demand

14. _____ describes the relocation by a company of a business process from one country to another -- typically an operational process, such as manufacturing such as accounting. Even state governments employ _____.

The term is in use in several distinct but closely related ways.

a. AAAI
b. Offshoring
c. A Stake in the Outcome
d. A4e

Chapter 12. Human Resource Management

15. _____ is subcontracting a process, such as product design or manufacturing, to a third-party company. The decision to outsource is often made in the interest of lowering cost or making better use of time and energy costs, redirecting or conserving energy directed at the competencies of a particular business, or to make more efficient use of land, labor, capital, (information) technology and resources. _____ became part of the business lexicon during the 1980s.
   a. Operant conditioning
   b. Opinion leadership
   c. Unemployment insurance
   d. Outsourcing

16. _____ refers to various methodologies for analyzing the requirements of a job.

The general purpose of _____ is to document the requirements of a job and the work performed. Job and task analysis is performed as a basis for later improvements, including: definition of a job domain; describing a job; developing performance appraisals, selection systems, promotion criteria, training needs assessment, and compensation plans.

   a. Hersey-Blanchard situational theory
   b. Work design
   c. Management process
   d. Job analysis

17. A _____ is a research instrument consisting of a series of questions and other prompts for the purpose of gathering information from respondents. Although they are often designed for statistical analysis of the responses, this is not always the case. The _____ was invented by Sir Francis Galton.
   a. Mystery shoppers
   b. Questionnaire construction
   c. Structured interview
   d. Questionnaire

18. A _____ is a quantitative research method commonly employed in survey research. The aim of this approach is to ensure that each interviewee is presented with exactly the same questions in the same order. This ensures that answers can be reliably aggregated and that comparisons can be made with confidence between sample subgroups or between different survey periods.
   a. Structured interview
   b. Questionnaire construction
   c. Questionnaire
   d. Mystery shoppers

Chapter 12. Human Resource Management

19. _____ are a method of interviews where questions can be changed or adapted to meet the respondent's intelligence, understanding or belief. Unlike a structured interview they do not offer a limited, pre-set range of answers for a respondent to choose, but instead advocate listening to how each individual person responds to the question.

The method to gather information using this technique is fairly limited, for example most surveys that are carried out via telephone or even in person tend to follow a structured method.

 a. A Stake in the Outcome
 b. AAAI
 c. A4e
 d. Unstructured interviews

20. Performance Testing covers a broad range of engineering or functional evaluations where a material, product, system emphasis is on the final measurable performance characteristics.

Performance testing can refer to the assessment of the performance of a human examinee. For example, a behind-the-wheel driving test is a _____ of whether a person is able to perform the functions of a competent driver of an automobile.

 a. 1990 Clean Air Act
 b. Reverse engineering
 c. 28-hour day
 d. Performance test

21. The term _____ in logic applies to arguments or statements.

An argument is valid if and only if the truth of its premises entails the truth of its conclusion, it would be self-contradictory to affirm the premises and deny the conclusion. The corresponding conditional of a valid argument is a logical truth and the negation of its corresponding conditional is a contradiction.

 a. Simplification
 b. Fuzzy logic
 c. 1990 Clean Air Act
 d. Validity

22. _____ is a process for determining and addressing needs, or gaps between current conditions and desired conditions organizations it is known as community needs analysis. It involves identifying material problems/deficits/weaknesses and advantages/opportunites/strengths, and evaluating possible solutions that take those qualities into consideration.

a. 33 Strategies of War
b. Needs assessment
c. 28-hour day
d. 1990 Clean Air Act

23. In the field of human resource management, _____ is the field concerned with organizational activity aimed at bettering the performance of individuals and groups in organizational settings. It has been known by several names, including employee development, human resource development, and learning and development.

Harrison observes that the name was endlessly debated by the Chartered Institute of Personnel and Development during its review of professional standards in 1999/2000.

a. Person specification
b. Performance appraisal
c. Revolving door syndrome
d. Training and development

24. There are two types of _____ relationships: formal and informal. Informal relationships develop on their own between partners. Formal _____, on the other hand, refers to assigned relationships, often associated with organizational _____ programs designed to promote employee development or to assist at-risk children and youth.

a. Fix it twice
b. Mentoring
c. Real Property Administrator
d. Human resource management system

25. _____ is the experience that a person has working, or working in a specific field or occupation.

The phrase is sometimes used to mean a type of volunteer work that is commonly intended for young people -- often students -- to get a feel for professional working environments. This usage is common in the United Kingdom, while the American equivalent is intern.

a. Work experience
b. Career break
c. Job fair
d. TDY

26. _____ is a method by which the job performance of an employee is evaluated _____ is a part of career development.

_____s are regular reviews of employee performance within organizations

Generally, the aims of a _____ are to:

- Give feedback on performance to employees.
- Identify employee training needs.
- Document criteria used to allocate organizational rewards.
- Form a basis for personnel decisions: salary increases, promotions, disciplinary actions, etc.
- Provide the opportunity for organizational diagnosis and development.
- Facilitate communication between employee and administraton
- Validate selection techniques and human resource policies to meet federal Equal Employment Opportunity requirements.

A common approach to assessing performance is to use a numerical or scalar rating system whereby managers are asked to score an individual against a number of objectives/attributes. In some companies, employees receive assessments from their manager, peers, subordinates and customers while also performing a self assessment.

a. Human resource management
b. Personnel management
c. Progressive discipline
d. Performance appraisal

27. _____ describes the situation when output from (or information about the result of) an event or phenomenon in the past will influence the same event/phenomenon in the present or future. When an event is part of a chain of cause-and-effect that forms a circuit or loop, then the event is said to 'feed back' into itself.

_____ is also a synonym for:

- _____ signal; the information about the initial event that is the basis for subsequent modification of the event.
- _____ loop; the causal path that leads from the initial generation of the _____ signal to the subsequent modification of the event.

_____ is a mechanism, process or signal that is looped back to control a system within itself. Such a loop is called a _____ loop.

a. Positive feedback
b. 1990 Clean Air Act
c. Feedback loop
d. Feedback

Chapter 12. Human Resource Management

28. A _____ is a set of categories designed to elicit information about a quantitative or a qualitative attribute. In the social sciences, common examples are the Likert scale and 1-10 _____ s in which a person selects the number which is considered to reflect the perceived quality of a product.

A _____ is an instrument that requires the rater to assign the rated object that have numerals assigned to them.

a. Spearman-Brown prediction formula
b. Polytomous Rasch model
c. Thurstone scale
d. Rating scale

29. A chief executive officer (_____) or chief executive is one of the highest-ranking corporate officer (executive) or administrator in charge of total management. An individual selected as President and _____ of a corporation, company, organization, or agency, reports to the board of directors. In internal communication and press releases, many companies capitalize the term and those of other high positions, even when they are not proper nouns.
a. CEO
b. Chief executive officer
c. Portfolio manager
d. Director of communications

30. _____ is how top executives of business corporations are paid. This includes a basic salary, bonuses, shares, options and other company benefits. Over the past three decades, _____ has risen dramatically beyond the rising levels of an average worker's wage.
a. Executive compensation
b. Evidence-based management
c. Association management company
d. Anti-leadership

31. The field of _____ looks at the relationship between management and workers, particularly groups of workers represented by a union.

_____ is an important factor in analyzing 'varieties of capitalism', such as neocorporatism, social democracy, and neoliberalism

a. Industrial relations
b. Informal organization
c. Organizational effectiveness
d. Overtime

32. The _____ is a 1935 United States federal law that limits the means with which employers may react to workers in the private sector that organize labor unions, engage in collective bargaining, and take part in strikes and other forms of concerted activity in support of their demands. The Act does not, on the other hand, cover those workers who are covered by the Railway Labor Act, agricultural employees, domestic employees, supervisors, independent contractors and some close relatives of individual employers.

It was in a context of severe economic troubles that the Wagner Act came into effect.

a. 28-hour day
b. National Labor Relations Act
c. 1990 Clean Air Act
d. 33 Strategies of War

33. The American Federation of Labor and Congress of Industrial Organizations, commonly _____, is a national trade union center, the largest federation of unions in the United States, made up of 65 national and international unions (including Canadian), together representing more than 10 million workers. It was formed in 1955 when the AFL and the CIO merged after a long estrangement. From 1955 until 2005, the _____'s member unions represented nearly all unionized workers in the United States.
a. United Mine Workers
b. A Stake in the Outcome
c. AFL-CIO
d. A4e

34. In organized labor, _____ is the method whereby workers organize together (usually in unions) to meet, converse, and negotiate upon the work conditions with their employers normally resulting in a written contract setting forth the wages, hours, and other conditions to be observed for a stipulated period. It is the practice in which union and company representatives meet to negotiate a new labor contract. In various national labor and employment law contexts, the term _____ takes on a more specific legal meaning. In a broad sense, however, it is the coming together of workers to negotiate their employment.
a. Paid time off
b. Labour law
c. Labor rights
d. Collective bargaining

35. An arbitral tribunal (or arbitration tribunal) is a panel of one or more adjudicators which is convened and sits to resolve a dispute by way of arbitration. The tribunal may consist of a sole _____, or there may be two or more _____s, which might include either a chairman or an umpire. The parties to a dispute are usually free to agree the number and composition of the arbitral tribunal.
   a. AAAI
   b. A Stake in the Outcome
   c. Arbitrator
   d. A4e

Chapter 13. Motivation and Performance 67

1. Clayton Paul Alderfer is an American psychologist who further expanded Maslow's hierarchy of needs by categorizing the hierarchy into his _____ Alderfer categorized the lower order needs (Physiological and Safety) into the Existence category. He fit Maslow's interpersonal love and esteem needs into the relatedness category. The growth category contained the Self Actualization and self esteem needs.

Alderfer also proposed a regression theory to go along with the _____. He said that when needs in a higher category are not met then individuals redouble the efforts invested in a lower category need.

   a. ERG theory
   b. Adam Smith
   c. Abraham Harold Maslow
   d. Alvin Neill Jackson

2. In law, _____ is the term to describe a partnership between two or more parties.

In England a number of statutes on the subject have been passed, the chief being the Bastardy Act of 1845, and the Bastardy Laws Amendment Acts of 1872 and 1873. The mother of a bastard may summon the putative father to petty sessions within twelve months of the birth (or at any later time if he is proved to have contributed to the child's support within twelve months after the birth), and the justices, as after hearing evidence on both sides, may, if the mother's evidence be corroborated in some material particular, adjudge the man to be the putative father of the child, and order him to pay a sum not exceeding five shillings a week for its maintenance, together with a sum for expenses incidental to the birth, or the funeral expenses, if it has died before the date of order, and the costs of the proceedings.

   a. Adam Smith
   b. Affiliation
   c. Abraham Harold Maslow
   d. Affiliation

3. In game theory, an _____ is a set of moves or strategies taken by the players, or their payoffs resulting from the actions or strategies taken by all players. The two are complementary in that given knowledge of the set of strategies of all players, the final state of the game is known, as are any relevant payoffs. In a game where chance or a random event is involved, the _____ is not known from only the set of strategies, but is only realized when the random event(s) are realized.
   a. A4e
   b. Outcome
   c. AAAI
   d. A Stake in the Outcome

Chapter 13. Motivation and Performance

4. _____ is about the mental processes regarding choice, or choosing. It explains the processes that an individual undergoes to make choices. In organizational behavior study, _____ is a motivation theory first proposed by Victor Vroom of the Yale School of Management.

   a. AAAI
   b. A Stake in the Outcome
   c. A4e
   d. Expectancy theory

5. Maslow's _____ is a theory in psychology, proposed by Abraham Maslow in his 1943 paper A Theory of Human Motivation, which he subsequently extended to include his observations of humans' innate curiosity.

   Maslow's _____ is predetermined in order of importance. It is often depicted as a pyramid consisting of five levels: the lowest level is associated with physiological needs, while the uppermost level is associated with self-actualization needs, particularly those related to identity and purpose. Deficiency needs must be met first. Once these are met, seeking to satisfy growth needs drives personal growth. The higher needs in this hierarchy only come into focus when the lower needs in the pyramid are met.

   a. 28-hour day
   b. 1990 Clean Air Act
   c. Hierarchy of needs
   d. 33 Strategies of War

6. _____ was developed by Frederick Herzberg, a psychologist who found that job satisfaction and job dissatisfaction acted independently of each other. _____ states that there are certain factors in the workplace that cause job satisfaction, while a separate set of factors cause dissatisfaction.

   a. Need for Achievement
   b. 1990 Clean Air Act
   c. Two-factor theory
   d. Need for power

7. _____ refers to an individual's desire for significant accomplishment, mastering of skills, control, or high standards. The term was introduced by the psychologist, David McClelland.

   _____ is related to the difficulty of tasks people choose to undertake.

a. Need for achievement
b. Need for power
c. 1990 Clean Air Act
d. Two-factor theory

8. The _____ is a term that was popularised by David McClelland and describes a person's need to feel a sense of involvement and 'belonging' within a social group. However, it should be recognised that McClellend's thinking was strongly influenced by the pioneering work of Henry Murray who first identified underlying psychological human needs and motivational processes (1938.) It was Murray who set out a taxonomy of needs, including Achievement, Power and Affiliation - and placed these in the context of an integrated motivational model.
   a. SESAMO
   b. Strong-Campbell Interest Inventory
   c. Polynomial conjoint measurement
   d. Need for affiliation

9. _____ is a term that was popularized by renowned psychologist David McClelland in 1961. However, it should be recognized that McClellend's thinking was strongly influenced by the pioneering work of Henry Murray who first identified underlying psychological human needs and motivational processes (1938.) It was Murray who set out a taxonomy of needs, including Achievement, Power and Affiliation - and placed these in the context of an integrated motivational model.
   a. Need for Achievement
   b. Two-factor theory
   c. Need for power
   d. 1990 Clean Air Act

10. _____ attempts to explain relational satisfaction in terms of perceptions of fair/unfair distributions of resources within interpersonal relationships. _____ is considered as one of the justice theories, It was first developed in 1962 by John Stacey Adams, a workplace and behavioral psychologist, who asserted that employees seek to maintain equity between the inputs that they bring to a job and the outcomes that they receive from it against the perceived inputs and outcomes of others (Adams, 1965.) The belief is that people value fair treatment which causes them to be motivated to keep the fairness maintained within the relationships of their co-workers and the organization.
   a. Equity theory
   b. AAAI
   c. A Stake in the Outcome
   d. A4e

11. _____ has become one of the most popular theories in organizational psychology.

Chapter 13. Motivation and Performance

Goal setting has been a formula used for acheivement since the early 1800s. The form and pattern has cahanged drastically over the years and there is still much debate as to what is the most efective pattern to follow.

a. Corporate Culture
b. Human relations
c. Job satisfaction
d. Goal-setting theory

12. _____ is the use of consequences to modify the occurrence and form of behavior. _____ is distinguished from classical conditioning (also called respondent conditioning, or Pavlovian conditioning) in that _____ deals with the modification of 'voluntary behavior' or operant behavior. Operant behavior 'operates' on the environment and is maintained by its consequences, while classical conditioning deals with the conditioning of respondent behaviors which are elicited by antecedent conditions.
    a. Unemployment insurance
    b. Occupational Safety and Health Administration
    c. Outsourcing
    d. Operant conditioning

13. _____ refers to training in different ways to improve overall performance. It takes advantage of the particular effectiveness of each training method, while at the same time attempting to neglect the shortcomings of that method by combining it with other methods that address its weaknesses.

Cross training is employee-employer field means, training employees to do one another's work.

   a. 28-hour day
   b. 1990 Clean Air Act
   c. 33 Strategies of War
   d. Cross-training

14. In operant conditioning, _____ occurs when an event following a response causes an increase in the probability of that response occurring in the future. Response strength can be assessed by measures such as the frequency with which the response is made (for example, a pigeon may peck a key more times in the session), or the speed with which it is made (for example, a rat may run a maze faster.) The environment change contingent upon the response is called a reinforcer.
   a. Diminishing Manufacturing Sources and Material Shortages
   b. Reinforcement
   c. Historiometry
   d. Meetings, Incentives, Conferences, and Exhibitions

Chapter 13. Motivation and Performance

15. _____ is learning that occurs as a function of observing, retaining and, in the case of imitation learning, replicating novel behavior executed by others. It is most associated with the work of psychologist Albert Bandura, who implemented some of the seminal studies in the area and initiated social learning theory. It involves the process of learning to copy or model the action of another through observing another doing it.
    a. A Stake in the Outcome
    b. AAAI
    c. A4e
    d. Observational learning

16. _____ is the theory that people learn new behavior through overt reinforcement or punishment, or via observational learning of the social actors in their environment. If people observe positive, desired outcomes in the observed behavior, they are more likely to model, imitate, and adopt the behavior themselves.

    _____ is derived from the work of Gabriel Tarde (1843-1904) which proposed that social learning occurred through four main stages of limitation:

    - close contact,
    - imitation of superiors,
    - understanding of concepts,
    - role model behaviour

    It consists of 3 parts observing, imitating, and reinforcements

    Julian Rotter moved away from theories based on psychosis and behaviourism, and developed a learning theory. In Social Learning and Clinical Psychology (1954), Rotter suggests that the effect of behaviour has an impact on the motivation of people to engage in that specific behaviour.

    a. 28-hour day
    b. 33 Strategies of War
    c. 1990 Clean Air Act
    d. Social learning theory

17. _____ is the belief that one is capable of performing in a certain manner to attain certain goals. It is a belief that one has the capabilities to execute the courses of actions required to manage prospective situations. Unlike efficacy, which is the power to produce an effect (in essence, competence), _____ is the belief (whether or not accurate) that one has the power to produce that effect.
    a. 1990 Clean Air Act
    b. 28-hour day
    c. 33 Strategies of War
    d. Self-efficacy

Chapter 13. Motivation and Performance

18. _____ is a term describing performance-related pay, most frequently in the context of educational reform. It provides bonuses for workers who perform their jobs better, according to measurable criteria. In the United States, policy makers are divided on whether _____ should be offered to public school teachers, as is commonly the case in the United Kingdom.
   a. Real wage
   b. Profit-sharing agreement
   c. Performance-related pay
   d. Merit pay

19. An _____ is a call option on the common stock of a company, issued as a form of non-cash compensation. Restrictions on the option (such as vesting and limited transferability) attempt to align the holder's interest with those of the business' shareholders. If the company's stock rises, holders of options experience a direct financial benefit.
   a. Employee stock option
   b. A Stake in the Outcome
   c. AAAI
   d. A4e

20. A _____ is a form of periodic payment from an employer to an employee, which may be specified in an employment contract. It is contrasted with piece wages, where each job, hour or other unit is paid separately, rather than on a periodic basis.

    From the point of a view of running a business, _____ can also be viewed as the cost of acquiring human resources for running operations, and is then termed personnel expense or _____ expense.

   a. Training and development
   b. Human resources
   c. Human resource management
   d. Salary

21. In finance, an _____ is a contract between a buyer and a seller that gives the buyer the right--but not the obligation-- to buy or to sell a particular asset (the underlying asset) at a later day at an agreed price. In return for granting the _____, the seller collects a payment (the premium) from the buyer. A call _____ gives the buyer the right to buy the underlying asset; a put _____ gives the buyer of the _____ the right to sell the underlying asset.
   a. AAAI
   b. A4e
   c. A Stake in the Outcome
   d. Option

22. _____, when used as a special term, refers to various incentive plans introduced by businesses that provide direct or indirect payments to employees that depend on company's profitability in addition to employees' regular salary and bonuses. In publicly traded companies these plans typically amount to allocation of shares to employees.

The _____ plans are based on predetermined economic sharing rules that define the split of gains between the company as a principal and the employee as an agent.

   a. Federal Wage System
   b. Wage
   c. Profit sharing
   d. Living wage

Chapter 14. Leadership

1. _____ has been described as the 'process of social influence in which one person can enlist the aid and support of others in the accomplishment of a common task'. A definition more inclusive of followers comes from Alan Keith of Genentech who said '_____ is ultimately about creating a way for people to contribute to making something extraordinary happen.'

_____ is one of the most salient aspects of the organizational context. However, defining _____ has been challenging.

   a. Situational leadership
   b. 1990 Clean Air Act
   c. Leadership
   d. 28-hour day

2. The 'business case for _____', theorizes that in a global marketplace, a company that employs a diverse workforce (both men and women, people of many generations, people from ethnically and racially diverse backgrounds etc.) is better able to understand the demographics of the marketplace it serves and is thus better equipped to thrive in that marketplace than a company that has a more limited range of employee demographics.

An additional corollary suggests that a company that supports the _____ of its workforce can also improve employee satisfaction, productivity and retention.

   a. Trademark
   b. Diversity
   c. Virtual team
   d. Kanban

3. The _____ is a leadership theory in the field of organizational studies developed by Robert House in 1971 and revised in 1996. The theory that a leader's behavior is contingent to the satisfaction, motivation and performance of subordinates. The revised version also argues that the leader engage in behaviors that complement subordinate's abilities and compensate for deficiencies.
   a. Path-goal theory
   b. Human relations
   c. Corporate Culture
   d. Sociotechnical systems

4. _____ refers to increasing the spiritual, political, social or economic strength of individuals and communities. It often involves the empowered developing confidence in their own capacities.

The term Human _____ covers a vast landscape of meanings, interpretations, definitions and disciplines ranging from psychology and philosophy to the highly commercialized Self-Help industry and Motivational sciences.

a. A Stake in the Outcome
b. AAAI
c. A4e
d. Empowerment

5. _____ is individual power based on a high level of identification with, admiration of, or respect for the powerholder.

Nationalism, Patriotism, Celebrities and well-respected people are examples of _____ in effect.

_____ is one of the Five Bases of Social Power, as defined by Bertram Raven and his colleagues[1] in 1959.

a. 28-hour day
b. 33 Strategies of War
c. 1990 Clean Air Act
d. Referent power

6. _____ of the learning curve effect and the closely related experience curve effect express the relationship between equations for experience and efficiency or between efficiency gains and investment in the effort. The experience of 'learning curves' was first observed by the 19th Century German psychologist Hermann Ebbinghaus according to the difficulty of memorizing varying numbers of verbal stimuli, and subsequent learning about the complex processes of learning are discussed in the

.

The rule used for representing the learning curve effect states that the more times a task has been performed, the less time will be required on each subsequent iteration.

a. Distribution
b. Models
c. Point biserial correlation coefficient
d. Spatial Decision Support Systems

7. _____ is a leadership style that defines as leadership that creates voluble and positive change in the followers. A transformational leader focuses on 'transforming' others to help each other, to look out for each other, be encouraging, harmonious, and look out for the organization as a whole. In this leadership, the leader enhances the motivation, moral and performance of his follower group.

a. Transformational leadership
b. Polynomial conjoint measurement
c. SESAMO
d. Strong-Campbell Interest Inventory

8. _____ is a term used to classify a group leadership theories that inquire the interactions between leaders and followers. A transactional leader focuses more on a series of 'transactions'. This person is interested in looking out for oneself, having exchange benefits with their subordinates and clarify a sense of duty with rewards and punishments to reach goals.
a. 1990 Clean Air Act
b. 28-hour day
c. 33 Strategies of War
d. Transactional leadership

9. _____ , often measured as an _____ Quotient (EQ), is a term that describes the ability, capacity, skill or (in the case of the trait _____ model) a self-perceived ability, to identify, assess, and manage the emotions of one's self, of others, and of groups. Different models have been proposed for the definition of _____ and disagreement exists as to how the term should be used. Despite these disagreements, which are often highly technical, the ability _____ and trait _____ models (but not the mixed models) are enjoying considerable support in the literature and have successful applications in many different domains.
a. AAAI
b. A Stake in the Outcome
c. A4e
d. Emotional intelligence

Chapter 15. Effective Groups and Teams

1. _____ is the term used to describe a situation where different entities cooperate advantageously for a final outcome. Simply defined, it means that the whole is greater than the sum of the individual parts. Although the whole will be greater than each individual part, this is not the concept of _____.

    a. 28-hour day
    b. 1990 Clean Air Act
    c. 33 Strategies of War
    d. Synergy

2. The phrase _____, according to the Organization for Economic Co-operation and Development, refers to 'creative work undertaken on a systematic basis in order to increase the stock of knowledge, including knowledge of man, culture and society, and the use of this stock of knowledge to devise new applications [sic]'

    New product design and development is more than often a crucial factor in the survival of a company. In an industry that is fast changing, firms must continually revise their design and range of products. This is necessary due to continuous technology change and development as well as other competitors and the changing preference of customers.

    a. 28-hour day
    b. 1990 Clean Air Act
    c. 33 Strategies of War
    d. Research and development

3. The _____ is a standardized, on-scene, all-hazard incident management concept. It is a management protocol originally designed for emergency management agencies in the United States which was later federalized there. It has since been adopted by agencies in other countries.

    a. A4e
    b. AAAI
    c. Incident Command Structure
    d. A Stake in the Outcome

4. A _____ -- also known as a geographically dispersed team -- is a group of individuals who work across time, space, and organizational boundaries with links strengthened by webs of communication technology. They have complementary skills and are committed to a common purpose, have interdependent performance goals, and share an approach to work for which they hold themselves mutually accountable. Geographically dispersed teams allow organizations to hire and retain the best people regardless of location.

    a. Kanban
    b. Virtual team
    c. Risk management
    d. Trademark

Chapter 15. Effective Groups and Teams

5. _____ is a dynamic of being mutually and physically responsible to and sharing a common set of principles with others. This concept differs distinctly from 'dependence' in that an interdependent relationship implies that all participants are emotionally, economically, ecologically and or morally 'interdependent.' Some people advocate freedom or independence as a sort of ultimate good; others do the same with devotion to one's family, community, or society. _____ recognizes the truth in each position and weaves them together.

   a. A4e
   b. A Stake in the Outcome
   c. AAAI
   d. Interdependence

6. The goal of most research on _____ is to learn why and how small groups change over time. To do this, researchers examine patterns of change and continuity in groups over time. Aspects of a group that might be studied include the quality of the output produced by a group, the type and frequency of its activities, its cohesiveness, the existence of conflict, etc.

   a. 28-hour day
   b. Group development
   c. 1990 Clean Air Act
   d. 33 Strategies of War

7. _____ has been described as the 'process of social influence in which one person can enlist the aid and support of others in the accomplishment of a common task'. A definition more inclusive of followers comes from Alan Keith of Genentech who said '_____ is ultimately about creating a way for people to contribute to making something extraordinary happen.'

   _____ is one of the most salient aspects of the organizational context. However, defining _____ has been challenging.

   a. 28-hour day
   b. 1990 Clean Air Act
   c. Situational leadership
   d. Leadership

8. In the social psychology of groups, _____ is the phenomenon of people making less effort to achieve a goal when they work in a group than when they work alone. This is seen as one of the main reasons groups are sometimes less productive than the combined performance of their members working as individuals.

   - Ringelmann, Max : 1913

Research began in 1913 with Max Ringelmann's study. He found that when he asked a group of men to pull on a rope, that they did not pull as hard, or put as much effort into the activity, as they did when they were pulling alone.

a. Social loafing
b. Personal space
c. Self-enhancement
d. Machiavellianism

Chapter 16. Promoting Effective Communication

1. _____, e-commuting, e-work, telework, working from home (WFH), or working at home (WAH) is a work arrangement in which employees enjoy flexibility in working location and hours. In other words, the daily commute to a central place of work is replaced by telecommunication links. Many work from home, while others, occasionally also referred to as nomad workers or web commuters utilize mobile telecommunications technology to work from coffee shops or myriad other locations.

   a. 33 Strategies of War
   b. 1990 Clean Air Act
   c. Telecommuting
   d. 28-hour day

2. _____ is the process of testing or tracking (monitoring) how end-users interact with a website or web application. _____ is often used by businesses to ensure that their customers are able to access their online applications and perform actions such as searching, online shopping, checking an account balance, or simply researching.

   Monitoring is essential to ensure that a website is available to users and downtime is minimized.

   a. 1990 Clean Air Act
   b. 28-hour day
   c. 33 Strategies of War
   d. Website monitoring

3. _____ is a subfield of the larger discipline of communication studies. _____, as a field, is the consideration, analysis, and criticism of the role of communication in organizational contexts.

   The field traces its lineage through business information, business communication, and early mass communication studies published in the 1930s through the 1950s.

   a. Organizational communication
   b. AAAI
   c. A Stake in the Outcome
   d. A4e

4. An _____ is a private computer network that uses Internet technologies to securely share any part of an organization's information or operational systems with its employees. Sometimes the term refers only to the organization's internal website, but often it is a more extensive part of the organization's computer infrastructure and private websites are an important component and focal point of internal communication and collaboration.

   An _____ is built from the same concepts and technologies used for the Internet, such as client-server computing and the Internet Protocol Suite (TCP/IP.)

a. A Stake in the Outcome
b. Intranet
c. AAAI
d. A4e

5. _____ is a recursive process where two or more people or organizations work together in an intersection of common goals -- for example, an intellectual endeavor that is creative in nature--by sharing knowledge, learning and building consensus. _____ does not require leadership and can sometimes bring better results through decentralization and egalitarianism. In particular, teams that work collaboratively can obtain greater resources, recognition and reward when facing competition for finite resources._____ is also present in opposing goals exhibiting the notion of adversarial _____, though this is not a common case for using the term.
 a. 1990 Clean Air Act
 b. 28-hour day
 c. Collaboration
 d. Collectivism

Chapter 17. Managing Conflict, Politics, and Negotiation

1. _____ is a state of discord caused by the actual or perceived opposition of needs, values and interests between people working together. Conflict takes many forms in organizations. There is the inevitable clash between formal authority and power and those individuals and groups affected.
   a. Organizational conflict
   b. A Stake in the Outcome
   c. A4e
   d. AAAI

2. _____ refers to the long-term management of intractable conflicts. It is the label for the variety of ways by which people handle grievances--standing up for what they consider to be right and against what they consider to be wrong. Those ways include such diverse phenomena as gossip, ridicule, lynching, terrorism, warfare, feuding, genocide, law, mediation, and avoidance.
   a. 1990 Clean Air Act
   b. 33 Strategies of War
   c. Conflict management
   d. 28-hour day

3. _____ is a recursive process where two or more people or organizations work together in an intersection of common goals -- for example, an intellectual endeavor that is creative in nature--by sharing knowledge, learning and building consensus. _____ does not require leadership and can sometimes bring better results through decentralization and egalitarianism. In particular, teams that work collaboratively can obtain greater resources, recognition and reward when facing competition for finite resources. _____ is also present in opposing goals exhibiting the notion of adversarial _____, though this is not a common case for using the term.
   a. Collaboration
   b. 28-hour day
   c. Collectivism
   d. 1990 Clean Air Act

4. An arbitral tribunal (or arbitration tribunal) is a panel of one or more adjudicators which is convened and sits to resolve a dispute by way of arbitration. The tribunal may consist of a sole _____, or there may be two or more _____s, which might include either a chairman or an umpire. The parties to a dispute are usually free to agree the number and composition of the arbitral tribunal.
   a. A Stake in the Outcome
   b. A4e
   c. AAAI
   d. Arbitrator

5. _____, in psychology, are goals that are achieved by the contribution and co-operation of two or more people, with individual goals that are normally in opposition to each other, working together.

Muzafer Sherif (1954) performed a study involving a group of boys at a camp that were in opposition to one another, one named Eagles, one named the Rattlers, in a zero-sum situation. The opposing groups had strong negative feelings towards each other, resulting in hostile actions such as 'garbage wars'.

a. 33 Strategies of War
b. 28-hour day
c. 1990 Clean Air Act
d. Superordinate goals

Chapter 18. Using Advanced Information Technology to Increase Performance

1. A _____ is a subset of the overall internal controls of a business covering the application of people, documents, technologies, and procedures by management accountants to solving business problems such as costing a product, service or a business-wide strategy. _____s are distinct from regular information systems in that they are used to analyze other information systems applied in operational activities in the organization. Academically, the term is commonly used to refer to the group of information management methods tied to the automation or support of human decision making, e.g. Decision Support Systems, Expert systems, and Executive information systems.
    a. 28-hour day
    b. Strategic information system
    c. 1990 Clean Air Act
    d. Management information system

2. _____ is one of the managerial functions like planning, organizing, staffing and directing. It is an important function because it helps to check the errors and to take the corrective action so that deviation from standards are minimized and stated goals of the organization are achieved in desired manner. According to modern concepts, _____ is a foreseeing action whereas earlier concept of _____ was used only when errors were detected. _____ in management means setting standards, measuring actual performance and taking corrective action.
    a. Control
    b. Schedule of reinforcement
    c. Turnover
    d. Decision tree pruning

3. _____ Management is the succession of strategies used by management as a product goes through its _____. The conditions in which a product is sold changes over time and must be managed as it moves through its succession of stages.

    The _____ goes through many phases, involves many professional disciplines, and requires many skills, tools and processes.

    a. Strategic Alliance
    b. Job hunting
    c. Golden handshake
    d. Product life cycle

4. _____ constitute a class of computer-based information systems including knowledge-based systems that support decision-making activities.

    _____ are a specific class of computerized information systems that supports business and organizational decision-making activities. A properly-designed _____ is an interactive software-based system intended to help decision makers compile useful information from raw data, documents, personal knowledge, and/or business models to identify and solve problems and make decisions.

Chapter 18. Using Advanced Information Technology to Increase Performance

a. Spatial Decision Support Systems
b. 1990 Clean Air Act
c. 28-hour day
d. Decision support systems

5. _____ is the intelligence of machines and the branch of computer science which aims to create it. Major _____ textbooks define the field as 'the study and design of intelligent agents,' where an intelligent agent is a system that perceives its environment and takes actions which maximize its chances of success. John McCarthy, who coined the term in 1956, defines it as 'the science and engineering of making intelligent machines.'

The field was founded on the claim that a central property of human beings, intelligence--the sapience of Homo sapiens--can be so precisely described that it can be simulated by a machine.

a. A4e
b. AAAI
c. A Stake in the Outcome
d. Artificial intelligence

6. An _____ is software that attempts to reproduce the performance of one or more human experts, most commonly in a specific problem domain, and is a traditional application and/or subfield of artificial intelligence. A wide variety of methods can be used to simulate the performance of the expert however common to most or all are 1) the creation of a so-called 'knowledgebase' which uses some knowledge representation formalism to capture the Subject Matter Experts (SME) knowledge and 2) a process of gathering that knowledge from the SME and codifying it according to the formalism, which is called knowledge engineering. _____s may or may not have learning components but a third common element is that once the system is developed it is proven by being placed in the same real world problem solving situation as the human SME, typically as an aid to human workers or a supplement to some information system.

a. A4e
b. AAAI
c. A Stake in the Outcome
d. Expert system

7. _____ are a class of electronic meeting systems, a collaboration technology designed to support meetings and group work. _____ are distinct from computer supported cooperative work (CSCW) technologies as _____ are more focused on task support, whereas CSCW tools provide general communication support.

_____ were referred to as a Group Support System (GSS) or an electronic meeting system since they shared similar foundations.

Chapter 18. Using Advanced Information Technology to Increase Performance

a. Hoshin Kanri
b. Learning organization
c. 1990 Clean Air Act
d. Group decision support systems

8. _____ is a company-wide computer software system used to manage and coordinate all the resources, information, and functions of a business from shared data stores.

An _____ system has a service-oriented architecture with modular hardware and software units and 'services' that communicate on a local area network. The modular design allows a business to add or reconfigure modules (perhaps from different vendors) while preserving data integrity in one shared database that may be centralized or distributed.

a. A Stake in the Outcome
b. AAAI
c. A4e
d. Enterprise resource planning

9. _____ is a form of multi-valued logic derived from fuzzy set theory to deal with reasoning that is approximate rather than precise. In contrast with binary sets having binary logic, also known as crisp logic, the _____ variables may have a membership value of only 0 or 1. Just as in fuzzy set theory with _____ the set membership values can range (inclusively) between 0 and 1, in _____ the degree of truth of a statement can range between 0 and 1 and is not constrained to the two truth values {true (1), false (0)} as in classic propositional logic.

a. Validity
b. Simplification
c. 1990 Clean Air Act
d. Fuzzy logic

10. _____ describes commerce transactions between businesses, such as between a manufacturer and a wholesaler, or between a wholesaler and a retailer. Contrasting terms are business-to-consumer (B2C) and business-to-government (B2G.)

The volume of B2B transactions is much higher than the volume of B2C transactions.

a. Category management
b. Product bundling
c. Market environment
d. Business-to-business

Chapter 18. Using Advanced Information Technology to Increase Performance

11. _____, commonly known as e-commerce, consists of the buying and selling of products or services over electronic systems such as the Internet and other computer networks. The amount of trade conducted electronically has grown extraordinarily with widespread Internet usage. The use of commerce is conducted in this way, spurring and drawing on innovations in electronic funds transfer, supply chain management, Internet marketing, online transaction processing, electronic data interchange (EDI), inventory management systems, and automated data collection systems.

   a. A Stake in the Outcome
   b. A4e
   c. Online shopping
   d. Electronic Commerce

12. Business-to-consumer describes activities of businesses serving end consumers with products and/or services.

    An example of a _____ transaction would be a person buying a pair of shoes from a retailer. The transactions that led to the shoes being available for purchase, that is the purchase of the leather, laces, rubber, etc.

    a. PEST analysis
    b. Market environment
    c. Green marketing
    d. B2C

13. A _____ is a formal relationship between two or more parties to pursue a set of agreed upon goals or to meet a critical business need while remaining independent organizations.

    Partners may provide the _____ with resources such as products, distribution channels, manufacturing capability, project funding, capital equipment, knowledge, expertise, or intellectual property. The alliance is a cooperation or collaboration which aims for a synergy where each partner hopes that the benefits from the alliance will be greater than those from individual efforts.

    a. Farmshoring
    b. Golden parachute
    c. Strategic alliance
    d. Process automation

14. The _____ of an edge is $c_f(u, v) = c(u, v) - f(u, v)$. This defines a residual network denoted $G_f(V, E_f)$, giving the amount of available capacity. See that there can be an edge from u to v in the residual network, even though there is no edge from u to v in the original network.

a. 1990 Clean Air Act
b. Residual capacity
c. 33 Strategies of War
d. 28-hour day

15. A _____ is a contemporary apporach to organizational design. It is an organization that is not defined by, or limited to, the horizontal, vertical, or external boundaries imposed by a predefined structure. This term was coined by former GE chairman Jack Welch because he wanted to eliminate vertical and horizontal boundaries within GE and break down external barriers between the company and its customers and suppliers.

a. Business Roundtable
b. Headquarters
c. Boundaryless organization
d. Chief risk officer

16. _____ comprises a range of practices used in an organisation to identify, create, represent, distribute and enable adoption of insights and experiences. Such insights and experiences comprise knowledge, either embodied in individuals or embedded in organisational processes or practice.

An established discipline since 1991, _____ includes courses taught in the fields of business administration, information systems, management, and library and information sciences.

a. Knowledge management
b. 1990 Clean Air Act
c. 28-hour day
d. 33 Strategies of War

17. _____ refers to a (generally IT based) system for managing knowledge in organizations for supporting creation, capture, storage and dissemination of information. It can comprise a part (neither necessary or sufficient) of a Knowledge Management initiative.

The idea of a _____ is to enable employees to have ready access to the organization's documented base of facts, sources of information, and solutions.

a. 33 Strategies of War
b. 28-hour day
c. 1990 Clean Air Act
d. Knowledge management system

Chapter 18. Using Advanced Information Technology to Increase Performance 89

18. The _____ (Situation, Task, Action, Result) format is a job interview technique used by interviewers to gather all the relevant information about a specific capability that the job requires. This interview format is said to have a higher degree of predictability of future on-the-job performance than the traditional interview.

- Situation: The interviewer wants you to present a recent challenge and situation in which you found yourself.
- Task: What did you have to achieve? The interviewer will be looking to see what you were trying to achieve from the situation.
- Action: What did you do? The interviewer will be looking for information on what you did, why you did it and what were the alternatives.
- Results: What was the outcome of your actions? What did you achieve through your actions and did you meet your objectives. What did you learn from this experience and have you used this learning since?

a. Phrase completion
b. Star
c. Competency-based job descriptions
d. Rasch models

ANSWER KEY

Chapter 1
1. b   2. d   3. a   4. d   5. c   6. d   7. d   8. d   9. b   10. c
11. b   12. d   13. d

Chapter 2
1. c   2. b   3. d   4. b   5. c   6. d   7. d   8. d   9. a   10. b
11. d   12. a   13. d   14. d   15. a   16. b   17. d   18. a   19. b   20. a

Chapter 3
1. b   2. b   3. a   4. d   5. d   6. a   7. d   8. b   9. c   10. d
11. d   12. c   13. d   14. a   15. a   16. a

Chapter 4
1. d   2. d   3. c   4. b   5. a   6. c

Chapter 5
1. d   2. d   3. c   4. b   5. d   6. c   7. b   8. d   9. a   10. a
11. c   12. c   13. d   14. d   15. b   16. d

Chapter 6
1. b   2. d   3. a   4. b   5. d   6. a   7. d   8. b   9. d   10. c
11. b   12. d   13. d

Chapter 7
1. a   2. c   3. d   4. d   5. b   6. d   7. d   8. d   9. d   10. d
11. d   12. d   13. d   14. a   15. c   16. b   17. d

Chapter 8
1. a   2. d   3. c   4. c   5. d   6. c   7. d   8. d   9. c   10. b
11. d   12. c   13. d   14. d   15. b

Chapter 9
1. a   2. d   3. c   4. b   5. b   6. d   7. b   8. b   9. d   10. d
11. b   12. d   13. d   14. d   15. c   16. c   17. b   18. c   19. a

Chapter 10
1. c   2. d   3. d   4. c   5. d   6. a   7. b   8. d   9. a   10. d
11. d   12. d   13. b   14. d   15. b   16. d   17. d   18. d   19. d

Chapter 11
1. b   2. d   3. c   4. d   5. c   6. d   7. b   8. d   9. d   10. c
11. a   12. a

ANSWER KEY

Chapter 12
1. d   2. c   3. d   4. d   5. d   6. b   7. d   8. d   9. b   10. d
11. c   12. b   13. d   14. b   15. d   16. d   17. d   18. a   19. d   20. d
21. d   22. b   23. d   24. b   25. a   26. d   27. d   28. d   29. a   30. a
31. a   32. b   33. c   34. d   35. c

Chapter 13
1. a   2. d   3. b   4. d   5. c   6. c   7. a   8. d   9. c   10. a
11. d   12. d   13. d   14. b   15. d   16. d   17. d   18. d   19. a   20. d
21. d   22. c

Chapter 14
1. c   2. b   3. a   4. d   5. d   6. b   7. a   8. d   9. d

Chapter 15
1. d   2. d   3. c   4. b   5. d   6. b   7. d   8. a

Chapter 16
1. c   2. d   3. a   4. b   5. c

Chapter 17
1. a   2. c   3. a   4. d   5. d

Chapter 18
1. d   2. a   3. d   4. d   5. d   6. d   7. d   8. d   9. d   10. d
11. d   12. d   13. c   14. b   15. c   16. a   17. d   18. b

www.ingramcontent.com/pod-product-compliance
Lightning Source LLC
Chambersburg PA
CBHW081846230426
43669CB00018B/2845